Created Being

Created Being

Expanding Creedal Christology

Rebecca L. Copeland

BAYLOR UNIVERSITY PRESS

© 2020 by Baylor University Press
Waco, Texas 76798

All Rights Reserved. No part of this publication may be reproduced, stored in a retrieval system, or transmitted, in any form or by any means, electronic, mechanical, photocopying, recording, or otherwise, without the prior permission in writing of Baylor University Press.

Unless otherwise stated, Scripture quotations are from the New Revised Standard Version Bible, copyright 1989, Division of Christian Education of the National Council of the Churches of Christ in the United States of America. Used by permission. All rights reserved.

Cover and book design by Kasey McBeath
Cover image: Sankofa bird

Hardcover ISBN: 978-1-4813-1302-5
Library of Congress Control Number: 2020936972

Printed in the United States of America on acid-free paper with a minimum of thirty percent recycled content.

To Bogey

A Truly Beloved Creature of God

CONTENTS

Acknowledgments		ix
Preface		xi
1	Christological Divides	1
2	What's an *Ousia*?	13
3	Truly Created, Truly Creator	33
4	And God Became a Creature	63
5	Created Together	77
Notes		91
Bibliography		133
Index		143

ACKNOWLEDGMENTS

I would like to thank all of those without whom this book would not have been possible. First and foremost that means thanking my parents, Dick and Mary Lee Copeland, whose love, enthusiasm, and support for my work has not wavered since I left my stable government job in the middle of a recession to move to Georgia to begin my theological education. My heartfelt thanks go to Jennifer Dalton, Jacob Pruett, and their family for being my conversation partners as I worked out many of these ideas, a sounding board during my first halting attempts to articulate them, and a refuge when I could not think or talk about theology anymore. The faculty at Candler School of Theology and the Graduate Division of Religion at Emory University were indispensable in the development of this project. I could not begin to name each one who helped shape me into the theologian I am today, for fear of leaving one out. Three, in particular, however, must be thanked personally. Steve Kraftchick was an excellent mentor through the ThM program, a lifeline who helped to preserve my sanity during the early years of the PhD program, and a detail-oriented reader of my dissertation. For his assistance, I will be forever grateful. Bobbi Patterson became a mentor during my first year in the Ph.D. program, and continued the adventure through the formation of the Religion and Ecology Collaborative. She is one of the greatest influences on my pedagogical formation, and a friend I will treasure for the rest of my life. Finally, Ian McFarland first inspired my love for theology as a master's student, challenging me to always ask deeper questions and seek fuller explanations. He continued to challenge me throughout the development of this project, and I will always treasure every "Good work" I have ever received from him. I can only wish everyone had the privilege of an advisor as intellectually stimulating and supportive as mine.

This project would not have been completed, nor taken the form it finally has, without my colleagues at Boston University School of Theology. Mary Elizabeth Moore has been a supportive conversation partner as we talked through the ideas in these pages and those yet to come. Shelly Rambo took on the role of mentoring me as a junior colleague, became a genuine friend, and played the indispensable role of introducing me to her publisher. Carey Newman first saw the possibilities of this project, and brought me on board with Baylor University Publishing, and Cade Jarrell has kindly and conscientiously supported me through all of the anxiety of a first-time author. My thanks go to all at Baylor who have brought this project to fruition.

Finally, I would like to thank my colleagues Brady Beard and David Carr for their friendship, their wisdom, their biblical expertise, and their intellectual gifts. My ideas become clearer and better through our conversations. I can't imagine doing this without you. #sharedbrain

PREFACE

The Sankofa bird, whose long neck curves to look over its back while holding an egg in its beak, illustrates the Akan proverb, "Se wo were fi na wosam kofa a yenki." This translates, "It is not taboo to go back and fetch what you forgot."[1] Symbolizing the critical retrieval of tradition for the enrichment of future generations, the Sankofa bird is a fitting image for the work of theologians throughout history.

Theologians draw on vast resources of tradition—both religious and secular—in speaking about God, humanity, and creation. The doctrines they propose are not entirely novel. They do not arise solely from the theologian's personal reflection or experiences, but are built on concepts inherited from those who have gone before. Those concepts are retrieved, preserved, amended, or expanded in order to be coherent with the world as the theologian encounters it. Some concepts are discarded when they seem to have outlived their usefulness. Others are brought forward and re-interpreted in the language of the day.[2]

When a crisis renders the old concepts problematic, there is a strong temptation to jettison them altogether and construct new ones. There is nothing shameful, however, in going back to fetch what has been forgotten. The concepts that laid the foundation for crumbling edifices might not be the problem. The bedrock can be sound even if what was built upon it was not strong enough to stand through the ages. Rather than seeking new ground upon which to build, theologians may need to tear down unsafe structures and rebuild on the same solid rock.

Separating what is sound, true, and in need of preservation from what is failing, deceptive, and ready to be discarded entails a process of critical retrieval.[3] This requires accurately diagnosing the problems that we face today and examining the traditions we have inherited to see how they do (and do not) contribute to those problems. Many theologians are engaged in such critical retrieval, drawing on ancient sources to address such varied topics as human sexuality, racism, and ecological degradation.[4] The present book is located within this stream of constructive theological work. As an act of retrieval, this project grants the resources of the Christian tradition deference, treating Scripture, the writings from ecumenical councils, and earlier theological works as the earnest attempts of faithful people to express their encounters with ultimate reality to the best of their respective abilities. Because it is also critical, however, it does not treat any such source as inerrant or free from the distortions that imperfect knowledge or implicit biases might introduce into such attempts.[5]

The problems theology must address today include increasing violence fueled by a resurgence of xenophobia, misogyny, and racism, and an ever-worsening ecological crisis, exacerbated by an anthropocentric disregard for the well-being of the other creatures upon whom human beings depend. These problems are rooted in how we understand ourselves in relationship to one another, to other creatures, and to God. For Christians, the doctrine of the incarnation, or how we understand the person of Jesus Christ, is arguably the most formative tradition for developing a proper orientation towards God and each other. Christian communities encourage their members to see Christ in one another, in the least of these they are meant to defend, and in the strangers that they meet. Many theologians argue that it is only in the person of Jesus Christ that we find the ideal representation of what it means to be properly human.[6] Because the doctrine of the incarnation provides the basis for forming Christian understandings of the relationship of human beings to all of reality, this work both examines the development of that doctrine for factors that exacerbate the problems of intra-human and ecological violence, and seeks to retrieve aspects of the doctrine that render the underlying causes of racism, misogyny, and harmful anthropocentrism untenable. After all, it is not taboo to go back for what has been left behind.

1
CHRISTOLOGICAL DIVIDES

> I believe in one Lord Jesus Christ,
> the Only Begotten Son of God,
> born of the Father before all ages.
> God from God, Light from Light,
> true God from true God,
> begotten, not made, consubstantial with the Father;
> through him all things were made.
> For us men and for our salvation
> he came down from heaven,
> and by the Holy Spirit was incarnate of the Virgin Mary,
> and became man.
> For our sake he was crucified under Pontius Pilate,
> he suffered death and was buried,
> and rose again on the third day
> in accordance with the Scriptures.
>
> —from the Nicene Creed

Each week Christians around the world recite the Nicene Creed, affirming their belief that Jesus Christ is "true God from true God" and also that he "came down from heaven . . . and became man." For Christians, this claim goes beyond assertions of divine immanence—that God is present to all parts of creation. Rather, it asserts that the divine Word entered the world *as* the particular person Jesus. Christians have traditionally also affirmed that the incarnation has an absolute, universal, and unique significance for God's creation. This affirmation, so central to the Christian faith, causes problems. It caused problems in 325 CE, when the First Council of Nicaea met to address christological disagreements, and it continues to cause problems today. The problems that this doctrine creates can be classified into three broad categories: justice, coherence, and plausibility challenges to the incarnation. Some argue that the doctrine is unjust because Christology has been deployed to support a variety of moral evils, including Christian patriarchy, colonialism, and environmental desecration. Some challenge the coherence of the incarnation, arguing that it is illogical to assert that one person could be both human and divine because humanity and divinity are characterized by mutually exclusive properties. Other critics argue that the plurality of religions in the world and the incomprehensible size of the universe render implausible the claim that the actions of one particular person in one particular time and place could be universally significant. These challenges are raised both severally and jointly, and each emphasizes different aspects of christological controversy.

JUSTICE CHALLENGES

In the 1960s some believed that the Catholic Church might change its policy on the ordination of women. As women took on larger roles in society more generally, Pope Paul VI acknowledged that women should also play a more important role in "the various fields of the Church's apostolate."[1] A decade later, however, the Vatican clarified that women still could not be ordained as priests *because Christ was a man* and there must be a "natural resemblance" between the priest and Christ.[2] The Vatican used the person of Jesus to justify the continued exclusion of women from the Catholic priesthood.

A portrait of Jesus with Caucasian features, long hair, and oftentimes blue eyes hangs in churches across the United States. This portrait has been reproduced more than 500 million times since Warner Sallman first sketched the *Head of Christ* in 1924.[3] Despite the fact that Jesus was born to a Jewish family in Palestine, the myth that he was a white man persists in cultures shaped by white supremacy. It remained alive and well in 2013 when then-Fox News anchor Megyn Kelly argued on national television that "Jesus was a white man . . . he was a historical figure, that's a verifiable fact."[4] Prominent figures bolster white supremacy by promoting the myth that Jesus was Caucasian.

In 2007 the Southern Baptist Convention urged the US government not to take action on the Fourth Assessment Report of the Intergovernmental Panel on Climate Change, but rather to "reject government-mandated reductions in greenhouse gas emissions" and other regulatory actions that might impede economic growth.[5] Ten years earlier, Calvin Beisner had provided evangelical Christians with christological grounds for this perspective when he argued that as "the restorer of mankind," Christ revealed what human beings "are destined to become."[6] Drawing from gospel accounts of Jesus stilling the storm and cursing a fig tree, Beisner argues that human beings should exercise similar dominion over nature, and that "man's increasing subjugation of nature (Gen. 1:28) is a good thing."[7] Many Christians use the actions of Jesus to justify damaging environmental exploitation.

The abuses that people have justified by appealing to Jesus lead many to doubt Christian claims about the incarnation. John Hick argues that the doctrine of the incarnation "is inherently liable to dangerous misuse by fallen human nature," and has been used to justify "colonial exploitation of the Third (or two-thirds) World" and "Western patriarchalism."[8] Mary Daly argues that the symbol of Jesus Christ is inherently deficient and should be abandoned.[9] John Cobb notes, "Many thoughtful believers are clear that they do not want to continue to make assertions about Jesus Christ that are anti-Jewish or sexist. . . . Many want to avoid, in general, language that appears to belittle the faith of people in other religious communities."[10] Because many assume that the doctrine of the incarnation itself justifies these injustices, some theologians are willing to forego Christian claims about Jesus altogether, while others sacrifice the narrowly defined doctrine of the incarnation in favor of an incarnational understanding of reality.[11] The doctrine itself, however, does not support the unjust uses that have been made of it.[12] These problems arise when certain characteristics of Jesus, whether real (such as his maleness) or imagined (his whiteness or affiliation with Western cultural norms), are treated as soteriologically significant. Such interpretations are based on assumptions that the characteristics of Jesus represent the best possible characteristics, or that those who share certain characteristics with Jesus are somehow closer to God than are other beings.[13] If the doctrine of the incarnation and claims about its universal significance can be redeemed, they must be separable from these assumptions.[14]

COHERENCE CHALLENGES

Although Christianity is paradoxical, it should not simply spout nonsense.[15] Yet critics claim that spouting nonsense is precisely what the doctrine of the incarnation does.[16] This is because philosophers and theologians understand divinity and humanity as characterized by complementary attributes. Some attributes, such as location in place and finitude in knowledge and power, are applicable to human beings, while their negations—omnipresence, omniscience, and omnipotence—are applicable to the divine. These attributes are understood to be mutually exclusive: nothing can possess both an attribute and its negation at the same time and in the same way. Thus, the argument goes, it is logically impossible to affirm that one person could be both divine and human at the same time.[17] If being divine means that one must possess some attribute X, and being human means that one must possess some attribute not-X, then it is incoherent to say that the same person could be both X and not-X at the same time.[18]

Challenges to the coherence of the incarnation are based on *a priori* definitions of divinity and humanity.[19] *A priori* definitions of divinity can be found in the lists of attributes that classical theism has found appropriate to attach to God, including: eternality, omnipotence, omniscience, omnipresence, self-existence, impeccability, impassibility, immutability, and goodness.[20] These characteristics are typical of the understanding, advanced by Anselm of Canterbury in the eleventh century, that God is "that than which nothing greater can be thought."[21] From this description, Anselm deduced that God is "whatever it is better to be than not to be," including self-existent, creator of all things, just, truthful, happy, percipient, omnipotent, merciful, impassible, living, wise, good, eternal, and unbounded.[22] This list is not simply an apophatic denial of limitations to the divine, but the positive attribution of certain characteristics to God, characteristics that can be called "great-making properties."[23] Under this line of reasoning, the divine attributes are all of those characteristics that it is better to possess than not to possess, and that can be possessed together. The greatness of these attributes is assumed to be self-evident: obviously it is greater to be impassible than to be passible, greater to be living than to be non-living, and greater to be unbounded than to be bounded.[24] According to those challenging the coherence of the incarnation, if Jesus is fully God, he must possess all of the great-making attributes that classical theism has assigned to God.

In contrast, humanity is defined as visible, comprehensible, limited, passible, localized to a place, mutable, contingent, peccable, and non-omniscient.[25] The majority of these characteristics are properties commonly held by all material beings; that is, the characteristics of visibility, comprehensibility, limitation, placed-ness, contingency, and non-omniscience are as applicable to all other material bodies as they are to human beings. Humans share the characteristics of mortality and passibility with all living beings. Only peccability, the capacity to sin, can arguably be limited to human beings alone among material beings, although those who allow that other beings also possess some form of freedom might include peccability among these shared characteristics as well.[26] If Jesus is fully human, then he must possess all of those attributes that characterize human existence.

Several characteristics from *a priori* definitions of humanity and divinity do seem to be logically incompatible.[27] If the doctrine of the incarnation can be redeemed from incoherence, it will need to re-examine *a priori* understandings of humanity and divinity, offer an understanding of human language in relationship to defining such natures, and advance an explanation of how these definitions are not incompatible.[28]

PLAUSIBILITY CHALLENGES

The final set of plausibility challenges rest on the belief that modern, or postmodern, understandings of the cosmos render unbelievable claims that one particular person, living in one particular place and time, is uniquely and universally salvific. Plausibility challenges are primarily based on two developments: greater exposure to other cultures and religions, and a better understanding of the enormity of the cosmos (and with that, the possibility of sentient life on other planets). In light of the Enlightenment's focus on the equality of human beings and its related critique of special (or limited) revelation, critics argue that these developments render the doctrine implausible if the salvific effects of the incarnation are not equally available to all.

The populations of the world have not had equal access to the special revelation of the incarnation, and many believe this lack of equity makes salvation on the basis of it unjust. Christian claims to possess unique or superior revelation in the Gospels lead to a disparagement of other religious traditions, whether or not this slight is intentional. Christian teaching that "outside the church (or outside Christianity) there is no salvation" leads many in religiously plural contexts to reject Christianity rather than believe that God condemns moral individuals of other faiths for not living according to a revelation they have either never received or been culturally conditioned to disbelieve.

Additionally, the universe as we understand it at the beginning of the twenty-first century is undeniably different than the understanding held by the earliest Christians. Not only has the Ptolemaic, geocentric cosmology of the ancient world been supplanted by a heliocentric model that places the sun at the center of the solar system, the universe is much larger than previously imagined—composed of billions of galaxies, each containing billions of stellar systems. The earth is not the center of the cosmos, as premodern belief systems held, but a tiny part of it. This recognition has led many to argue that the idea that God would become incarnate on this single planet for the lifespan of one single man is as erroneous as the idea that the sun orbits the earth.[29] The reasoning behind this objection is not nearly as clear as its proponents assume, however. The difference in magnitude between the universe as it was understood two thousand years ago and as it is understood now does not explain how the claim for the universal significance of one man's life was once believable and yet no longer is.[30] The earth itself is very large, and it is far beyond the ability of any human being to establish a personal relationship with every inhabitant of it. Nevertheless, many who argue that our current knowledge of the cosmos calls the doctrine of the incarnation into question do not deny that God could be personally interested in every human being. It remains unclear, therefore, how current cosmologies generate a context for salvation that outstrips the abilities of God.[31]

This argument may take the ancient view that human beings are the center of creation as fundamental to Christianity. Modern cosmology and evolutionary biology undermine such anthropocentric assumptions, and challengers appear to be arguing that if human beings are not the center or goal of the universe then the doctrine of the incarnation automatically fails. According to this reasoning, the incarnation is only plausible if human beings are more important to God than are other created beings. Such importance was plausible in a smaller universe, or one in which everything was ordered around human beings, or in which human beings had a special origin separate from other living beings. With scientific discoveries of the size and ordering of the universe, and about the evolutionary emergence of human beings through the same processes that govern the development of all life on this planet, such assumptions that human beings are held in particular divine esteem are undermined.[32]

Critics of the plausibility of the incarnation also argue that the possibility of sentient life on other planets undermines the doctrine. Since extraterrestrial life would not have access to the revelation that Jesus brought, their condemnation would be as unfair as that of human beings who have never heard of Jesus.[33] This leads some to entertain the idea of multiple incarnations—one for each planet, or possibly for each species of sentient life.[34] The assumption governing this line of argumentation seems to be that extraterrestrial life would need access to *knowledge* of the incarnation in order for it to be effective.

Plausibility challenges are based on assumptions about how the incarnation is effective (through the revelation of particular knowledge), and about the significance of human beings (that incarnation as a human could be universally effective only if human beings are the lynchpin of creation). A Christology capable of answering these challenges must demonstrate that the significance of the incarnation is not dependent on human centrality or revelation alone. Instead, it will need to offer a metaphysical understanding of the efficacy of the incarnation that works through other means than cognitive appropriation of revealed truths.[35]

A DIFFERENT STARTING POINT

Many Christians hear these challenges and stop making the outrageous claim that Jesus is both God and man. Other Christians hear these criticisms and conclude that God must actually want men to rule over women, that God genuinely favors white people, that people of other faiths are in fact going to hell, and that environmental protection is indeed idolatry.[36] Christological claims cause problems. Nevertheless, both the solution of abandoning such claims altogether and the solution of accepting the problems those claims cause as a matter of faith are based on flawed reasoning that equates how groups have used the doctrine of the incarnation with the doctrine itself. Christians do not have to repudiate the doctrine, nor do they have to accept the abuses that have been justified by appeals to it.

It is helpful to recognize that these problems and the recent responses to them are not in fact new. In lieu of claiming that Jesus is both God and man, many Christians make compromises, allowing that Jesus functions as a symbol of the divine and need not be thought of as a real human being at all, or claiming that he was an extraordinary man and inspired by God, but not really divine. These are options the church has entertained and rejected in the past: the first, associated with Docetists, posited that Jesus feigned humanity in order to reach human beings, but always remained impassibly divine; and the second, associated with Ebionites, held that Jesus was an inspired human being but not truly divine.[37] A docetic Christ meant Jesus was an unreliable representation of God, a deceiver who only feigned suffering while commanding his followers to take up their crosses and follow him. An Ebionite Christ might be a good teacher, but would be incapable of conferring the full breadth of salvation that Christians claimed Jesus brought. Both were rejected by the Council of Nicaea, which affirmed that Jesus Christ is "from the substance of the Father, God from God, light from light, true God from true God, begotten not made, consubstantial with the Father," and that he "came down and became incarnate, became human."[38] Nicaea was the first of the church's ecumenical councils, gatherings of bishops and others from the major dioceses in Christendom, convened in order to resolve theological controversies and issue doctrinal statements. These ecumenical councils produced what has come to be called "conciliar Christology": a body of statements about what the church did and did not find acceptable to say about Jesus Christ.[39] This does not mean that their statements were meant to fully explicate the doctrine of the incarnation. Instead, they set the boundaries for future christological reflection.[40]

The First Council of Nicaea, in 325 CE, was soon followed by the councils of Constantinople (381), Ephesus (431), and Chalcedon (451). Each council refined the understanding of Jesus offered. Whereas Nicaea opposed Arian teaching by affirming the genuine divinity of Jesus Christ as "consubstantial with the Father" and also that he "came down and became incarnate, became human, suffered and rose up on the third day," Constantinople added that he "became incarnate from the holy Spirit and the virgin Mary, became human and was crucified on our behalf under Pontius Pilate; he suffered and was buried and rose up on the third day in accordance with scriptures."[41] Competing councils at Ephesus took up the debates between Cyril, the bishop of Alexandria, and Nestorius, the bishop of Constantinople, with each council issuing contradictory rulings.[42] The aftermath of this controversy continued over the following years and was resolved (for some) when the Council of Chalcedon upheld the Cyrilline Council of Ephesus and issued a fuller explication of the person of Christ. Chalcedon acknowledged Jesus Christ, "in two natures which undergo no confusion, no change, no division, no separation; at no point was the difference between the natures taken away through the union, but rather the property of both natures is preserved and comes together into a single person and a single subsistent being; he is not parted or divided into two persons, but is one and the same."[43] These statements encapsulate the early church's affirmation that Jesus *is* both fully human and fully divine, but they do not explain *how* he could be both. They do not proclaim that certain human beings are closer to God or of more value to God. They do not *necessitate* the justice, coherence, or plausibility problems that interpretations of these statements have created, but by leaving so many questions unanswered, they did make such problems possible.

Because the councils do not offer a fully fleshed-out Christology of their own, but do provide insight into what the early church found unacceptable to say about Christ, they remain a useful starting point for christological reflection that intends to develop their claims in ways that do not lead to the problems identified. What follows is not a defense of the ecumenical councils from all attacks nor an attempt to prove that they were correct in all of their assertions.[44] Rather, it is an attempt to articulate a Christology that affirms with the councils that Jesus Christ was consubstantial with both the Father and with us, maintains the absolute and universal significance of the incarnation, and avoids the problems that have been associated with other christological developments.

In order to avoid the problems of injustice, incoherence, and implausibility that have plagued christological reflection, this investigation must begin with a different set of assumptions than those that have largely governed Chalcedonian Christology. The ecumenical councils, like almost all christological reflection since, began with soteriology, or claims about salvation.[45] The Council of Nicaea clearly states that the presumed purpose of the incarnation is "for us humans and for our salvation."[46] The claims pro-Nicene Christians made about who Jesus was were shaped by this assumption about what Jesus does. Concerned primarily with the human predicament and with human salvation, their doctrinal statements were shaped by anthropocentric assumptions that neglected the universal efficacy of the incarnation for all of creation. This is not to say that the implications of the incarnation for creation were never considered by early theologians. From biblical times to today, there have been advocates for a cosmic understanding of Christ as the one who is the creator, sustainer, redeemer, and goal of all things.[47]

Drawing from such diverse scriptural sources as Jewish wisdom literature, the prophets, apocalyptic literature, epistles, and the gospels, cosmic Christologies assert that the Word who becomes incarnate is both the source of all of creation and the pattern that knits it all together.[48] This enlarges the understanding of salvation that proponents of cosmic Christologies advance, expanding it beyond the forgiveness of human sin to the healing, restoration, and consummation of all of creation.[49] According to such Christologies, salvation cannot be thought of as salvation *from* the created world, but must always be considered as salvation *of* and *with* the created world.[50] In other words, for cosmic Christologies, salvation must be cosmic in scope as well. These claims do not give rise to the justice issues described. In the context of cosmic Christologies, those problems arise from the fact that even when the concept of salvation is expanded to encompass the entire cosmos, it is still shaped by anthropocentric assumptions about what salvation must be and about the centrality of human beings within creation.[51]

Early sources of cosmic Christologies understood salvation to be an ending of transience and mortality. Athanasius of Alexandria assumed that human beings alone of all creatures were made to "abide ever in blessedness" and be granted incorruption through their share in the image of God, and that the incarnation was necessary to overcome sin and return humanity to this special status.[52] Similarly, Gregory of Nyssa argued that through Christ's resurrection, "our mortal race begins its return to immortal life."[53] Even when modern theologians argue that mortality is not inherently evil, but a factor of life that seemingly must accompany sexual reproduction, it remains something from which we stand in need of rescue.[54] These definitions of salvation reflect a deeply human fear of death.[55]

Both defining salvation in ways that address particularly human concerns, rather than the concerns of all creatures, and limiting the work of the incarnation to human salvation automatically undermine the notion that it is universally significant.⁵⁶ To avoid these problems, a Christology that affirms the universal effectiveness of the incarnation needs to bracket concerns about human salvation in order to consider what the incarnation might mean for other members of creation.⁵⁷ This does *not* require denying that the incarnation accomplishes human salvation as well, but it does mean rethinking the "work" of the incarnation from a more inclusive perspective. Rather than starting from the foundational assumption that the purpose of the incarnation is for human salvation, this christological reflection begins from the foundational assumption that the incarnation affects every member of creation. From there it will explore whether the "us" with whom Jesus is said to be consubstantial might be considered expansively as including other members of creation, what it means to say that Jesus is consubstantial with creation, and how the Word becoming incarnate as a creature might affect all of creation.⁵⁸

This approach will raise objections based on certain long-standing assumptions about theological method and epistemological limitations. The division between the "immanent" and "economic" Trinity—how God is in Godself and how God is known in the world—is based on the epistemological divide that proclaims human beings can only know God in God's dealing with us.⁵⁹ This assumption means that any claims about God in Godself that are not based on God's activity in the world are purely speculative and overstep the epistemological boundaries placed on human knowledge. Without denying this assumption, theological reflection need not limit itself to consideration of human salvation if God's activity, including the incarnation, reaches beyond purely human concerns. If the incarnation affects all of creation, then all of creation is an acceptable locus for christological reflection.

Even if epistemological boundaries are not violated by taking all of creation into account, a second objection remains. Both Scripture and Christian tradition provide support for the idea that human beings are of central importance in creation and to God.⁶⁰ There is a presumption that the Word's becoming incarnate as a human being supports this idea that God values human beings more than other creatures.⁶¹ It might seem that setting human concerns and human salvation to the side in order to consider the efficacy of the incarnation for all of creation is inappropriate given this history. Of course, both Scripture and the vast majority of Christian tradition have provided support for the idea that men are of greater importance in creation and to God than are women, yet many theologians have found the androcentrism of both Scripture and the tradition inappropriate given the larger message of the gospel and have adjusted their interpretations accordingly. It is possible that an anthropocentric bias, similar to the androcentric bias that many have rejected, has distorted both the biblical text and the Christian tradition.[62] Exploration of Christology that (at least temporarily) sets aside concerns about human dignity is a needed correction for such distortion.

Scripture supports this setting aside concerns about one's personal dignity, as can be seen in Jesus' instructions on banquet etiquette in Luke 14:7-11. Dining with a leader of the Pharisees, Jesus observed the guests vying for the place of honor. He advised his followers to behave differently, not taking the seat of honor but rather taking the lowest place. He explained that if they took the place of honor but the host had invited someone more important to the banquet, then they would be publicly shamed when asked to give up their seats. On the other hand, if they took the lowest seat then their host might insist that they move to a higher seat, an honor that would impress all of those at the table. The recommended behavior is not simply an attempt to gather honor or avoid shame, but stems from an epistemological humility adopted by those who are not themselves the host of the event. As Jesus explained, "do not sit down at the place of honor, in case someone more distinguished than you has been invited *by your host*" (Luke 14:8, emphasis added). This passage indicates that Christians are dependent upon another for determination of honor (or value)—God, who is the host. Further, it offers advice on how to behave in the uncertainty created by this condition of dependence. Do not assume that you are the guest of honor; leave that for the host to decide. Foregoing the traditional assumption that human beings are the guests of honor at creation's banquet adopts the epistemic humility Jesus advises in Luke 14:7-11.

Recognizing and resisting the biases that place human beings—particularly privileged male human beings—in the seat of honor for theological reflection can build a bridge between liberal Christians who are willing to give up the doctrine of the incarnation, if necessary, in order to oppose injustice, and conservative Christians who are willing to accept injustice, if it is mandated by doctrine. Treating other members of creation as important sources for theological insight, this project is not simply a defense of creedal Christology from the objections that have been raised against it. Rather, it is a constructive theological proposal that honors the traditional claim that the incarnation is the defining event of created reality by reading the doctrine inclusively, that is, by claiming that in the incarnation the Word assumes created being. By expanding the doctrine beyond the more exclusive category of human being, the following chapters develop new ways of talking about created reality, the divine, and the relationship between the two. Doing so provides grounds for reconsidering all of creation in light of the incarnation, while also answering the justice, coherence, and plausibility challenges that have been raised against the doctrine. Having defined these challenges in the present chapter, chapter 2 sets forth historical, scientific, and theological justifications for reading the doctrine of the incarnation in terms of consubstantiality with all of creation, and demonstrates that doing so undermines justice challenges to the doctrine. Chapter 3 develops a provisional definition of created substance and demonstrates how Jesus Christ might coherently be understood to be both created and divine. Chapter 4 reconstructs a metaphysical understanding of the incarnation that demonstrates its universal and immediate effectiveness for all of creation, thus undermining plausibility challenges to the doctrine. Finally, chapter 5 examines the implications of this proposal for further theological and ethical development.[63]

Reorienting the initial christological inquiry from how Jesus saves us from the human condition to what the incarnation of the Word accomplishes for all of creation places Christology on different ground. Approaching Christology from this starting place reveals the anthropocentric biases that have shaped the development of christological claims, demonstrates how the biased development of those claims leads to the christological problems identified, and offers more fertile ground for developing a Christology that is both plausible and coherent, while also opposing injustice against any member of God's good creation.

2
WHAT'S AN *OUSIA*?

The first task of offering a (re)constructive christological proposal that opposes injustice against any member of creation involves ascertaining how the theological commitments underlying creedal claims support an inclusive understanding of the incarnation and identifying resources within those claims for opposing inequities. The proposal shaped by this examination then needs to be tested against both those creedal commitments and contemporary understandings of reality, including scientific, theological, and ethical understandings. In order to address inequities that have been justified by appealing to the incarnation, this will require reexamining the conciliar claim that Jesus Christ is "consubstantial with us."[1]

"Consubstantial" is not one of the more common words in the English language, but its Greek equivalent played a significant role in early christological debates. The Nicene Creed states that Jesus Christ is "consubstantial with the Father," and the definition of faith offered by the Council of Chalcedon adds that he is "consubstantial with us as regards his humanity."[2] This claim is the heart of the doctrine of the incarnation—that "for us and for our salvation" one who is consubstantial with God the Father became consubstantial with human beings. The question of whether the doctrine of the incarnation supports the injustices of Christian patriarchy, racism, and environmental degradation depends on how these phrases are interpreted. "Consubstantial with us" can be read exclusively as limiting the scope of the incarnation to the species of *Homo sapiens*, to those who descend from certain ancestral gene pools, or to those who are men. Alternatively, it can be read inclusively, as encompassing the entirety of creation, including but not limited to the entire population of *Homo sapiens*. Both church history and contemporary scientific knowledge indicate that the latter, inclusive reading is more legitimate.

The word that is translated "consubstantial" in the Nicene Creed is *homoousios* in the original Greek. *Homo* translates straightforwardly as "same," but *ousia* poses more of a conundrum. It is the noun form of the Greek verb for "to be" and is commonly translated into English as "being," "substance," or "essence." Each of these terms is open to a wide range of possible meanings.[3] They could refer to the actuality of a thing, "being" meaning that it really exists rather than existing only in potentiality. "Substance" could indicate the stuff out of which it is made. "Essence" might refer to the particular kind of thing it is, or what its "essential" characteristics are. What all of these various definitions have in common is that they refer to the appropriate classification of a thing—what it is, and in what category it belongs.

Like modern taxonomies, ancient thinkers used hierarchical systems for categorizing beings. Each more particular category was delineated by certain traits that the categorizers deemed significant. Although the term *ousia* was used in these systems of classification, it did not equate to one particular level of that categorization. It could instead be used to indicate any level of specificity between the individual existent thing and its *genus summum*.[4] Although ancient authors both understood distinctions between the more particular and the more general and used those distinctions in framing their own arguments, their use of *ousia* did not necessarily reflect those distinctions. Because *ousia* could refer to any level in their categorical hierarchy, modern interpreters need to engage the contexts in which the term is used to determine its precise meaning.

HISTORICAL DEVELOPMENT

The concept of *ousia* is grounded in questions about what something is. The early church was quickly confronted with questions about what Jesus Christ was. He was, most evidently, a human being. The testimony of Scripture and the apostolic fathers, however, agreed that he was also the Son of God. This created a categorical difficulty that was further confused by Jesus' statements that "I and the Father are one," and "the Father is greater than I" (John 10:30; 14:28). Based on these statements, Jesus might be the same thing as the Father, or he might be something lesser that shared some characteristics with the one true God, but lacked others. Christians found themselves defending their faith in the contexts of Greco-Roman philosophical schools and the Jewish faith, both of which had come to the conclusion that God was one, simple, not composed of different things, incorporeal, and not subject to growth or division. Yet Christians claimed that the Father and the Son were both worthy of worship and were both divine, while still claiming to worship the one God of Judaism. How they navigated this tension was governed to a large extent by what they understood to be necessarily implied by their claim that Jesus saves.[5]

Substance and Salvation

The early church understood the incarnation to be linked inextricably to salvation, and this belief determined what they found theologically acceptable to say about the incarnation. Acceptable answers to the question, "What is Jesus Christ?" had to include something that could impart salvation. Understanding what the early church meant when it claimed that Jesus was consubstantial with both the Father and us requires understanding how that church understood salvation.

This interpretive task is complicated by the fact that there was no single understanding of salvation in the early church—no more than there is a single understanding among Christians today. Some of the earliest theologians and Scripture writers mixed metaphors when talking about salvation: Jesus is the ransom that frees us from captivity, the thief that ties the strong man up, the man fighting for his people, the great physician who brings healing, the lamb who died for our sins, and the one who brings renewal and reconciliation. Such theologians did not use these metaphors competitively, but rather viewed them as complementary, layering one on top of the other in their attempts to describe the ineffable.[6] Without delving into an in-depth review of all of the writings on salvation from the first five centuries of the church, examining two influential examples provides a sketch of the soteriological background for the ecumenical councils that is capable of illuminating the metaphysical commitments behind conciliar christological statements.

Writing in opposition to second-century Gnosticism, Irenaeus of Lyons described the work of the incarnation in several different ways. In passages from the third and fifth books of *Against Heresies*, he described the work of Christ as overcoming the enemy of humanity, granting salvation, dispensing incorruptibility, reconciling humanity with God in friendship and adoption, destroying sin, redeeming humanity from death, bringing life to human beings, and conveying knowledge of the things of God.[7] Strikingly, two centuries later one of the staunchest defenders of Nicene Christianity, Athanasius of Alexandria, provided a similar description of the effects of the incarnation. In one paragraph from *On the Incarnation of the Word*, he describes the work of Christ in (at least) five different ways. According to Athanasius, in the incarnation Jesus Christ turns human beings from corruption to incorruption, renews the defaced image of God, brings immortality to mortal beings, teaches true knowledge of God, and satisfies the requirements of justice.[8] Although neither Irenaeus nor Athanasius found it necessary to separate their metaphors into any sort of typology, it is helpful to examine them in terms of four categories of soteriological models in order to explore the metaphysical assumptions underlying their christological understandings. These categories include martial, forensic, pedagogical, and therapeutic understandings of salvation.[9]

Martial models draw from notions of warfare.[10] According to these models, human beings lost the battle with sin and were captured by the enemy. Imprisoned, we stand in need of rescue by one who has not been captured. Jesus is the only human being who has not been defiled by sin. Thus, he is able to save humanity by winning our release from captivity, either through the payment of our ransom or by defeating the enemy in the larger battle.[11] Salvation consists in the liberation of humanity from captivity. Irenaeus' assertions that Christ overcomes the enemy, destroys sin, and redeems humanity from death all illustrate martial understandings of salvation.[12]

Forensic models are based on ideas of fault and recompense.[13] Any disobedience to the divine law is a fault deserving condemnation. Because all human beings have sinned, humanity stands under condemnation, alienated from God through disobedience. We need to be pardoned in order to be saved from our sentence. As the only human being that has not been alienated from God by sin, Jesus is the one who can stand before God to plead humanity's case. In this model, Jesus mediates reconciliation between God and humanity either by bearing humanity's sentence himself or by winning our pardon from God through his life of obedience. Athanasius' claim that Jesus pays the necessary debt explicitly invokes forensic understandings of salvation, while Irenaeus' mediatorial language about restoring friendship, concord, and communion implies such an understanding of salvation as removing the cause of ruptured relationship.[14]

In pedagogical models, the human predicament is one of ignorance. Originally created to know God, humanity's failure to do so threatens to thwart God's purposes. We need a teacher who can instruct us properly. As one with true knowledge of God, Jesus is able to be this teacher to humanity. He saves by conveying this knowledge and serving as a model for proper human life.[15] Both Irenaeus and Athanasius refer to Christ as the one who brings humanity true knowledge of God.[16]

Finally, therapeutic models treat human beings as gravely wounded, ill, or disfigured.[17] Although humanity was created in the image of God, sin so defaced that image that it is no longer recognizable. Humanity needs healing. Jesus is the one who possesses the power to cure the disease. In the therapeutic model, Jesus saves by healing wounds and restoring the image that has been defiled. Both Irenaeus and Athanasius invoke therapeutic understandings of salvation when they attribute the dispensing of incorruption and life (or immortality) to the work of Christ.[18]

In order for Jesus to be able to save, he must be something that is capable of defeating the enemy and worthy of pleasing God. He must be something that possesses both true knowledge of God and the ability to heal humanity of the wounds that sin has inflicted. In order for him to be able to do any of these things, Jesus must be something more than other captured, guilty, ignorant, and/or injured human beings. In order to save, Jesus must also be divine.[19] This belief, and its apparent conflict with the confession that God is one, led to the earliest Christian debates over the meaning of *homoousios*.

At the beginning of the fourth century, Arius, a priest in Alexandria, was concerned that treating Jesus as divine diminished the honor given to God the Father. He taught that, unlike the Father, "the Son has a beginning," and "before he was begotten or created or defined or established, he was not."[20] This teaching sparked a conflict with his bishop, Alexander of Alexandria, who argued instead that Scripture indicates that Jesus is eternally "the divinity of the Wisdom of the Word, which is Christ."[21] Although the Arian controversy is widely understood to revolve around the eternality or pre-existence of the Word, Arius and his opponents were also disagreeing about how to properly understand what Jesus was. The issue of whether he was co-eternal with the Father implicated questions of his *ousia* as well.

If there was a "before" when the Son "was not," from what substance did he come? Arius claimed that the Son was "from nothing" because he was "neither part of God nor from any substratum."[22] By this argument, Arius denied that the substance of the Son could be the same as the substance of God. In a letter defending this teaching to his bishop, Arius positioned himself as the defender of Christian orthodoxy against Gnosticism and other heretical teachings that the Son was an emanation, or an unacceptable division of God's unique oneness.[23] Working from the same materialistic perspective the Gnostics used, Arius argued that if the Son was from the same substance as God, then begetting the Son would divide or deplete God in some way.[24] For Arius, this left only the possibility that the Son's *ousia* was "from nothing," deriving its unique properties from God's will rather than from God's *ousia*. The rest of creation was also "from nothing," and so only God's will distinguished Jesus from everything else that was created. Arius' opponents rejected the claim that the Son was from nothing because this would place the Son on par with the rest of the created order, which is also from nothing.[25] These pre-Nicene debates indicate that there were two possible answers to the question of what the Son was, at least on the level of originating substance or *ousia*. The Son could be of the same substance as the Father or "from nothing."[26]

This debate over the substance of the Son caused enough upheaval that Emperor Constantine summoned the Council of Nicaea in 325 to settle the issue. The Council rejected Arius' solution, opting instead for Alexander's explanation that the Son is "from the *ousia* of the Father" and "*homoousios* with the Father."[27] They further ruled out any possibility that the Son was from any other *ousia* than the Father's, anathematizing "those who say that he came into being from things that were not, or from another *hypostasis* or *ousia*, affirming that the Son of God is subject to change or alteration."[28] Eusebius of Caesarea later explained the meaning of "*homoousios* with the Father," arguing that this clause "indicates that the Son of God bears no resemblance to originate creatures but that he is alike in every way only to the Father who has begotten and that he is not from any other *hypostasis* or substance but from the Father."[29] The context of the Arian debates illuminates Nicaea's use of the term *ousia*. They are not referring to a biological species, but rather use *ousia* to indicate a broad category related to the origin of being. They insisted that the only possible *ousiai* from which the Son could come are that of the Father or that of everything else that was created from nothing. The Council provides one of the earliest Christian articulations of the "infinite qualitative distinction" between God and human beings.[30] There are two *ousiai*, Creator and created, and an ontological divide lies between them. The Council clearly insisted that the Son's *ousia* was divine, "God from God, light from light, true God from true God."[31] Divine *ousia* was contrasted with all of creation, which Scripture says "came into being through him [the Word]" (John 1:3). This understanding of reality left no room for a third, intermediate *ousia*. Soteriologically, the claim that the Son was from the *ousia* of the Father guaranteed that the Son possessed the qualities and capacities necessary to rescue humanity from captivity, merit its pardon, teach it true knowledge, and cure its ills. According to Nicaea, it was in order to convey these gifts—that is, for our salvation—that the Son "became incarnate, became human, suffered, and rose up on the third day."[32]

Once Nicaea was affirmed by the second ecumenical council, held at Constantinople in 381, christological disputes turned from whether the Son was *homoousios* with the Father to how the humanity of Jesus conveyed to other human beings the benefits that the divine Son brought. In addition to being divine, in order for Jesus to be able to save, Christians needed to articulate how he was able to reach human beings. Early Christians assumed that he must be, in some way, consubstantial with us in order to convey salvation to us. Christ's humanity plays a key role in each of the models of salvation previously examined. Under the martial model, it was necessary for the Word to be disguised in human form in order for the enemy to either accept the ransom or engage in battle.[33] In forensic models, only a human being could discharge the sentence or merit the pardon for humanity.[34] In pedagogical models, human beings turned away from true knowledge of God to contemplate themselves. Thus, they could only be taught by one who was human as they were.[35] Finally, in therapeutic models, it was widely understood that the divine *ousia* was itself the healing balm that needed to be applied to perishing humanity.[36]

Although early Christians used a wide variety of models and metaphors in talking about the effects of the incarnation, there were common metaphysical assumptions underlying them all. First, all of humanity was connected in some way, or shared in some substance, such that the Word uniting itself with one human being could convey the benefits of that union to the rest of humanity. Second, divinity itself was the cure for all that ails humanity, such that divinity uniting with humanity achieves victory, reconciliation, education, and healing. To use a modern medical metaphor, divinity is the antibiotic that must come into contact with the pathogen harming humanity in order to eliminate it. Thus, conciliar Christology implicitly claims that what later came to be called the hypostatic union of divinity and humanity in the incarnation is the metaphysical mechanism by which Jesus saves. The Council of Chalcedon described this union as one in which Christ is "acknowledged in two natures which undergo no confusion, no change, no division, no separation," and in which "the property of both natures is preserved and comes together into a single person and a single subsistent being [*hypostasis*]."[37] Salvation was achieved not by God granting it to humanity from outside, but by the Word enacting it from within humanity.[38]

The Council of Nicaea's claim that the Word was *homoousios* with the Father and corresponding rejection of the possibility that the Word derived from created *ousia* carried an implicit affirmation that everything that is not God shares in created *ousia*. This first ecumenical pronouncement undermines any later hierarchization among the created order. Instead, it positions humanity in solidarity with the rest of the created cosmos, as envisioned by cosmic Christologies.[39]

Theological Anthropology

Despite this cosmic solidarity, the church was, and largely remains, focused on the salvation of human beings in particular. Therefore, the implications of Nicene logic for the rest of creation have been widely neglected. Debates over the character of the union between humanity and divinity in the person of Jesus quickly obscured the universal implications of Nicene logic. Rather than relying on Nicaea's metaphysical insight that all of creation shared in one *ousia*, early Christians adopted contemporary understandings of hierarchies within creation.[40] For example, Maximus the Confessor understood there to be five great divisions in reality: uncreated/created, intelligible/sensible, heaven/earth, paradise/inhabited world, and male/female. According to Maximus, the original human vocation was the unification of reality across these divides "as a kind of natural bond mediating between the universal poles through their proper parts, and leading into unity in itself those things that are naturally set apart from one another by a great interval."[41] Human beings were made up of parts, and some of those parts were "higher" or more god-like while others shared commonalities with the creatures "below." One early defender of Nicene Christianity, Apollinaris of Laodicea, proposed that the divine Logos replaced the highest human part, the mind, in Jesus.[42] The Word that was consubstantial with the Father joined the flesh of a human being, and so was able to bring salvation to humanity. Jesus was not a human being, however, because, "he is not coessential with humanity in his highest part."[43] Rather than recognizing that the mind as well as the body partook of created *ousia*, and therefore stood in need of whatever gifts the incarnation brought, Apollinaris assumed that the mind was higher than and separable from the bodily human condition. Gregory of Nazianzus represented the Cappadocian rejection of Apollinaris' solution most succinctly, arguing that "the unassumed is the unhealed, but what is united with God is also being saved."[44] According to this logic, if the Word did not assume a human mind, then the human mind could not be cured through the incarnation. Because the entire human being stood in need of a cure, the incarnation must include everything that makes a human being human.

When they came to examine what made human beings human, early Christians had a large philosophical tradition from which to draw. Aristotle had defined a human being as a living organism that is a featherless biped, possesses a sense of humor, is shaped by political instincts, has a capacity for recollection, and is rational.[45] These definitions highlight characteristics that were assumed to set human beings apart from all other species, but rationality in particular has been singled out to define human nature for millennia. In *De Anima*, Aristotle divided orders of material existence on the basis of whether a material body had a soul and what type of soul that body had. Inanimate material bodies (such as rocks) were differentiated from animate bodies because only the latter possessed a soul (*anima*).[46] Aristotle further distinguished between living bodies on the basis of how many of the five powers of the soul they possessed. These powers were "the nutritive, the appetitive, the sensory, the locomotive, and the power of thinking."[47] While plants had only the nutritive power, animals had nutritive, appetitive, sensory, and locomotive powers. Only human beings and "possibly another order like man or superior to him" had the power of thinking in addition to the other four powers.[48] This hierarchy of being was baptized into Christian understandings of the *imago Dei*, in which the scriptural claim that "God created humankind in his image" (Gen 1:27) was understood to indicate that *only* human beings possessed some characteristic that resembled God—most frequently assumed to be rationality.[49] In the thirteenth century this interpretation governed Aquinas' argument that humanity alone is made in the image of God:

> Now it is manifest that specific likeness follows the ultimate difference. But some things are like to God first and most commonly because they exist; secondly, because they live; and thirdly because they know or understand; and these last, as Augustine says, "approach so near to God in likeness, that among all creatures nothing comes nearer to Him." *It is clear, therefore, that intellectual creatures alone, properly speaking, are made in God's image.*[50]

Not only did the assumed distinctiveness of human rationality shape theological anthropology, it also played a significant role in christological debates. While plants possessed nutritive or vegetative souls, and animals possessed sensitive souls, human beings were thought to be alone among material creatures in possessing rational souls.[51] For this reason, it was necessary that Jesus possessed a rational human soul in order for the incarnation to be salvific.

By the fifth century, it was commonly accepted that human nature could be defined as a material body with a rational soul. This is evidenced by Cyril's use of an analogy to human nature to explain the incarnation. Analogies are useful tools for explaining something more mysterious in terms of its similarities to something that is more familiar or easier to understand, but analogical explanation is only helpful if one's interlocutors are already familiar with one part of the analogy. As Cyril explained, "a human being like ourselves cannot properly be divided into two *prosopa*, even though he is regarded as consisting of a soul and a body, but in a single human being with a single identity. The same is also true with regard to Emmanuel . . . his *prosopon* is necessarily single."[52] He used the same analogy, arguing that a murderer who kills one person cannot be convicted of two murders, "even though that one person [killed] is perhaps conceived of as being from soul and body and the nature of the component parts is not the same but different."[53] From these examples, Cyril argued that Jesus Christ was one person, even though he possessed two natures. If Cyril could use the union of body and soul in a human being to explain the mystery of the incarnation, then this understanding of human nature had to be generally known during his lifetime.

Cyril's assumption that human nature included both body and soul also lies behind his insistence that the Word assumed both a body and a rational soul.[54] Echoing Gregory of Nazianzus' soteriological concerns, Cyril cautioned that "if he had not . . . partaken of the same elements as we do, he would not have delivered human nature from the fault we incurred in Adam, nor would he have warded off the decay from our bodies, nor would he have brought to an end the power of the curse."[55] According to this line of reasoning, there is something ontologically distinctive about the rational souls of human beings, such that the assumption of a material body without the assumption of a rational soul would not have been able to cure humanity completely.[56]

This is why the Council of Ephesus expanded the christological definition offered by Nicaea and Constantinople I, adding that Jesus Christ is "perfect man *of a rational soul* and a body."[57] The Council of Chalcedon kept this addition, specifying that Jesus Christ is "perfect in humanity . . . truly man, *of a rational soul* and a body . . . *like us in all respects* except for sin."[58] Although the ecumenical councils used *ousia* to indicate the broadest categories of being (Creator or created), they became quite specific about Christ's humanity, defining it at the level of *infima species*. They defined true humanity in a way that highlighted what they assumed was the unique characteristic of human beings: the rational soul. Chalcedon's use of two *ousiai* followed Nicaea's logic, with two broad categories of created reality and divinity. However, those who wrote the Chalcedonian definition understood human nature to indicate something more exclusive, a principle that distinguished the human species from all the others.[59] This created a tension between the equalizing force of the two-*ousiai* formulation and the segregating impulse that emphasized those characteristics understood to make humanity unique.

OVERCOMING THEOLOGICAL DIVISIONS

The resulting marginalization of certain creatures, and the elevation of others, follows naturally, although not necessarily, from this segregating impulse. It follows Aristotelian physics in separating the animate from the inanimate, the animal from the vegetal, and human beings from other animals. It does not stop with humanity as the *infima species*, but continues to separate on the basis of race, nationality, and gender. Although there are genuine differences between individual creatures, and recognizing those differences is itself an inherent part of encountering individuals in the fullness of their created integrity, the segregating impulse becomes problematic when it insists on ordering one characteristic as higher (nearer to the divine, superior, or of greater value) than another, rather than simply recognizing it as different. Reclaiming Nicaea's two-*ousiai* framework counters this segregating impulse in three ways. It affirms an ontological distinction between the divine and creation, establishes human solidarity with the rest of creation, and demonstrates how the incarnation can be effective for all of creation without the mediation of any particular human being other than Jesus.

Turning first to the ontological divide between human beings and the divine, the Arian controversy established that there were fundamentally only two *ousiai* in all of reality: that of God, and that of all that God creates. Thus, human beings are created by God, but they are not from the *ousia* of God. This claim pushes against pantheistic claims that everything partakes of the divine, while simultaneously asserting that all things are immediately dependent upon God as their Creator. Because everything that is not of God's *ousia* is from nothing, by nature it would return to nothing but for God's creative providence.[60] This claim also guards against an idolatry that would elevate human beings, or particular human beings identified by gender, race, or some other characteristic, above the rest of creation, effectively trying to "play God" towards the rest of creation. Such elevation partakes of the Arian heresy both by taking away from the Son's unique dignity and by allowing that dignity to be bestowed upon other human beings. In contrast, Alexander argued that "our Lord, being Son of the Father by nature, is worshipped," and that human beings can only "become sons by adoption being shown a kindness by the Son."[61] The distinction of all of reality into two *ousiai*, coupled with the claim that Jesus is *homoousios* with the Father while we are not, defends against idolatry that impinges on Jesus' unique role as the mediator between Creator and creation.

This affirmation of the ontological divide between human beings and God undermines discriminatory exceptionalism by positioning all human beings in solidarity with the rest of creation. Gregory of Nyssa laid the foundation for this argument in his claim that Christ was born through normal human processes. Against those who "despise the method of human birth as something shameful and disgraceful," Gregory argued that evil alone is truly "unworthy of God."[62] In contrast to those who would argue that the incarnation as any creature other than a human being would be unworthy of God, he explained that

> Every created thing is equally inferior to the Most High who, by reason of his transcendent nature, is unapproachable. The whole universe is uniformly beneath his dignity. For what is totally inaccessible is not accessible

> to one thing and inaccessible to another. Rather does it transcend all existing things in equal degree. Earth is not more below his dignity, and heaven less. Nor do the creatures inhabiting each of these elements differ in this respect. . . . Everything is equally beneath the power that rules the universe. . . . If, then, everything equally falls short of this dignity, the one thing which really befits God's nature still remains, namely, to come to the aid of those in need.[63]

Although Gregory was specifically defending Jesus' birth from a woman as something that is no less worthy of God than the Word's incarnation as a man, the logic of his argument clearly undermines exceptionalism that holds that some human beings are more worthy of the incarnation than other created bodies would be. According to this argument, angels are not more worthy of being the recipients of the Word than are human beings, but by the same logic men are not more worthy than women, Caucasians are not more worthy than other ethnic groups, and human beings are not more worthy than frogs or field mice. Nicaea's insistence that there are two *ousiai* not only establishes an ontological distinction between God and everything else, but also undermines human hubris by placing all of humanity firmly on the "everything else" side of that distinction.

Finally, this claim of two *ousiai* undermines the anthropocentric tendency of many theologians to view the work of the incarnation as mediated by a particular group of human beings.[64] This tendency can be seen in the androcentric arguments that women cannot serve as priests and anthropocentric interpretations of scriptural passages that seem to imply that the fate of all of creation depends on human salvation (e.g., Rom 8:19-21).[65] The ecumenical councils asserted that the Son was *homoousios* with the Father because only that *ousia* possessed the cure for the ailments of creatures who came "from nothing." They also insisted that Jesus Christ was *homoousios* with us because only the union of the two *ousiai* could bring the cure to those who were perishing. However, if there are only two *ousiai*, this means men's *ousia* is the same as women's, and that human *ousia* is the same *ousia* as everything else that was created from nothing. If the incarnation affects human beings because the divine *ousia* is hypostatically united with created *ousia*, then it should affect all created beings equally. The ecumenical councils' arguments for two *ousiai* undermine androcentric, white supremacist, and anthropocentric assumptions. If there are only two *ousiai*, that of the Creator and that of all that is created, then whatever is accomplished in the incarnation is effective for all that partake in created *ousia*. This includes human beings, of course, but it includes the rest of material reality as well.

SCIENTIFIC INSIGHTS

Current scientific theories and research into cosmology, evolutionary biology, animal behavior, botany, and microbiology support the Nicene understanding that all created reality shares something, while also undermining the later exclusionary Christian emphasis on the particularity of humanity.[66] This research and these theories are appropriate resources for theological reflection because theology seeks understanding of the relationship between creation and Creator, or, in other words, a comprehensive understanding of reality as we experience it. This means that theologians should pay attention to the findings of other fields, even fields that themselves find theology completely irrelevant. In much the same way, a veterinarian must understand animal behavior, parasitology, biology, and chemistry in order to treat a sick animal, although a chemist need not take notice of animal behavior in order to amply pursue her own research in the field of chemistry. The more comprehensive approach should make use of the less comprehensive approach, but not vice versa. Therefore, the best information that the sciences can offer serves as a useful resource for theological reflection. Although scientists and theologians use different models and metaphors to speak about the origin of material reality and the current relationships between different material bodies, they paint a similar picture of the common origin and current interdependence of everything that exists.

The anthropocentric worldview that prioritizes the humanity of Christ, or particular characteristics of his humanity, is based on mistaken biological assumptions about the fixity of species and the origin of life. Although there have been other minority views throughout history, until Darwin's theory of natural selection was accepted species were assumed to be eternal, immutable categories by the vast majority of theologians, philosophers, and naturalists.[67] In contrast, Darwin offered an explanation of how contemporary species could have arisen from preceding generations:

> If... organic beings vary at all in the several parts of their organization, and I think this cannot be disputed; if there be... at some age, season, or year, a severe struggle for life, and this certainly cannot be disputed... if variations useful to any organic being do occur, assuredly individuals thus characterized will have the best chance of being preserved in the struggle for life; and from the strong principle of inheritance they will tend to produce offspring similarly characterized. This principle of preservation, I have called, for the sake of brevity, Natural Selection.[68]

Although Darwin did not know the genetic mechanism by which characteristics are passed along from parents to offspring, his theory was able to explain how species could both come into existence and go extinct in response to competition for resources. Darwin did not answer all questions about evolution, and debates continue over the details: whether it proceeds by the gradual and more or less continuous accumulation of small changes (the Modern Synthesis) or by rapid periods of speciation interspersed in long time periods with very little change (Punctuated Equilibrium); how natural selection works at the level of kinship groups, individual organisms, and species; the roles of genes themselves and of environmental factors in causing genetic changes; and the role of nonadaptive, or neutral mutations.[69] Despite these debates, the modern scientific community accepts that our species evolved from the first life forms, with creatures of greater complexity descending from simpler life forms.[70]

Evolution does not just undermine the notion of eternally fixed species, it destroys it. According to Platonic essentialism, the category of *infima species* correlates to the intelligible Form of that species, with each individual being reflecting that Form imperfectly. The Form was the ideal from which every physical manifestation fell short. In contrast, today a species can be defined as a population that can produce fertile offspring through interbreeding.[71] There is no ideal to which we can compare an individual being to decide whether it belongs in a species or not; the actual physical and mental attributes of individual members of the species may vary widely.[72] Naturalists have observed historically recent speciation in which genetic isolation and environmental pressures combine to lead to the evolution of two or more species from one common ancestral species. Daniel Dennett describes the *Larus* genus of herring gulls as one example of such observable speciation. Tracing the populations of herring gulls around the globe from England to North America, Russia, and back to England, the birds' appearance changes. Small variations add up, however, and in Great Britain where the circle meets one finds two different species, the herring and the lesser black-backed gull.[73] Under different environmental pressures, variations within a species can become differences of species. Although it is true that human beings are, generally, rational, featherless bipeds that live in communities and have the ability to laugh, there are certainly human beings with one or no legs, human beings that live in isolation from others, and human beings that lack a sense of humor, all without being expelled from the species of *Homo sapiens*. The herring gull, however, managed to diverge into two (to six) different species by circumnavigating the globe, and undergoing some minor physical alterations along the way. Species is a useful taxonomy for the study of living creatures, and (especially if some version of Punctuated Equilibrium is vindicated) the stability of species over time suggests the category is not without significance; but it does not seem to indicate an ultimate theological distinction between different categories of living beings.

Evolution is not the only scientific development that challenges premodern understandings of species as distinct groups governed by some eternal nature. Microbiology reveals that individual human beings are actually ecological communities, composed of a multitude of different species.[74] Of the nearly seventy trillion cells that make up an average human being, over half are genetically separate bacteria, eukaryotes, and viruses.[75] The makeup of our microbiota is influenced by human genetics, antibiotic use, and diet, but in turn it wields a great deal of influence over us as well.[76] Found throughout the body, these other-than-human creatures are responsible for human immune development, play a significant role in extracting nutrition from the foods that human beings consume, and have even been found to influence mood.[77] The abilities of the human body to digest food and fight off disease are products of the other species we play host to as well as our own genetically determined species-natures. In addition to sharing a common ancestry with every other living creature on earth through evolution, human beings are actually communities of trillions of different organisms. If human capacities are the result of symbiotic relationships among a community of organisms, then evaluations of the capacities of other species might need to take their larger symbiotic communities into account as well.[78]

Not only biology but also contemporary work in physical cosmology underscores the common origin and physical interdependence of everything that exists. According to the Big Bang theory, the universe began as a single point and has been expanding for approximately fifteen billion years.[79] Everything in the universe is subject to the same natural laws or physical forces.[80] As with evolution, there continues to be debate about the Big Bang theory, particularly over the ultimate fate of the universe. Nevertheless, the evidence indicates that the entire universe shares a common origin in the distant past. Everything comes from a common origin and shares in an interdependent community of kinship.[81] Modern science supports the implicit claims of the ecumenical councils that all material reality shares a common *ousia*, and continuing research undermines notions of a fixed and ontologically distinct nature possessed by humanity alone in all of creation.

Considering the materials out of which we are made, the origin from which we arose, and the forces that govern our physical existence, there are deep similarities between human beings and every other material body that exists. All living creatures can trace their genealogy back to the earliest, simplest life forms to emerge. Even beyond that, there are material bodies including viruses, proteins, and individual amino acids that seem to stand at the transition from the living to the non-living universe, exhibiting similarities to both. There is continuity between all material bodies, even as they differ in organization and activity.[82] The picture of the universe, material existence, and the development of life that the physical sciences have given us at the beginning of the twenty-first century coheres nicely with implications of the two-*ousiai* claim of Nicaea: every material body is of the same *ousia*.

ADDRESSING JUSTICE CHALLENGES

The theological payoff of recovering a two-*ousiai* Christology is that it provides a scientifically, historically, and theologically reasonable foundation for liberation critiques of Christian patriarchy, racism, colonialism, and environmental degradation. The logic of this argument builds upon the logic of feminist critiques of androcentric Christology, like those offered by Rosemary Radford Ruether and Elizabeth Johnson. While the human nature that the ecumenical councils claimed the Word assumed in Jesus Christ was described in sexually generic terms, the androcentric biases of the culture in which they made this claim assumed that his maleness was essential to the incarnation. As Rosemary Radford Ruether explains, this was due to an erroneous biological assumption that the man provided the form of the child, and that female children were therefore defective copies of the paternal form, "inferior in body, intelligence, and in moral self-control."[83] Therefore, the seemingly gender-neutral assertion that Christ is perfect (hu)man (*anthropon teleion*) is actually an assertion of Christ's maleness, when read in light of the reigning scientific beliefs of the time. The same androcentric assumptions that essentialized the maleness of Christ in turn used that maleness to bolster patriarchal hierarchies. The idea that the maleness of Christ was essential to the incarnation has been used to give theological validation to household hierarchies that subordinate women to men, to exclude women from ordained ministry, and to attenuate the efficacy of the incarnation for women.

This emphasis on one particular characteristic of the incarnation, Christ's maleness, works against the theological benefits gained by the ecumenical councils' claim of two *ousiai*. Although recognition that all of reality partakes of only two *ousiai* upholds an ontological distinction between God and men, androcentric emphasis on the maleness of Christ asserted a "necessary ontological connection" between the male person of Christ and the divine nature.[84] Essentializing Christ's maleness erodes the solidarity of the sexes in their common nature, created in the image of God. Feminist critics point out that the traditional christological language of Logos/Word reflects this division, since

Logos "was particularly related to the rational principle," and rationality was considered a masculine quality lacking in women.[85] Gregory of Nyssa's argument that all parts of creation are equally unworthy of the incarnation is quickly lost in arguments that men are more truly the image of God than are women.[86] Johnson argues that although the ecumenical councils explicitly assert that the hypostatic union is unconfused, "the androcentric imagination" communicates Jesus' maleness to the divine nature, another example of the circular logic of Christian patriarchy.[87] These androcentric assumptions simultaneously undercut the solidarity of the sexes in their common humanity and degrade women to second-class citizenship in the realm of human beings.

In addition to setting men apart from women and elevating men above the rest of the created order (including human women) by virtue of their rational resemblance to God, essentializing the maleness of Christ supports an idolatrous overreaching in which men are needed to mediate salvation to women. While the church has never excluded women from salvation altogether, its androcentric anthropology, reinforced by essentialized views of the maleness of Christ, made male human beings the mediators of that salvation—specifically through a priesthood that excludes women, and more generally through the role of male family members as the "heads" of women.[88] Proponents of this perspective look for support to scriptural passages like 1 Corinthians 11:3: "I want you to understand that Christ is the head of every man, and the husband is the head of his wife, and God is the head of Christ," which uses a man-as-microcosm argument to justify the veiling of women in worship. Now that prior biological errors have been corrected, women are understood to be fully human rather than imperfectly formed men, and now that more egalitarian worldviews recognizing the full humanity of women are dominant, any continued emphasis on the maleness of Christ actually threatens claims about his soteriological significance for women. Referring to the Cappadocian argument that "what is unassumed is unhealed," Johnson argues that if gender is essential to the incarnation, women remain unhealed because female sexuality remains unassumed.[89] If Jesus saves women, then his maleness cannot be a soteriologically significant characteristic of the incarnation.

Reformist feminist theologians have addressed this conundrum by simultaneously affirming the maleness of the person Jesus and arguing that maleness is no more essential to the incarnation than is his ethnicity, height, or hair color. Ruether argues that we need to be able to affirm all of the particularity required for Jesus Christ to have been truly human without treating any particular human characteristic as more soteriologically significant than one of its foregone alternatives.[90] Addressing the inappropriate emphasis that has been placed on

Jesus' maleness requires understanding that maleness in the same way that all of his other particular characteristics have been understood. These characteristics are part of Jesus' unique constitution as an individual material body, but they are not a barrier to his universal significance. Similarly, Johnson argues that all of Jesus' particularity needs to be understood using "a multipolar anthropology" that refuses to emphasize one particular characteristic as more significant than the others.[91] Johnson and Ruether respond to patriarchal assumptions about the maleness of Christ by emphasizing the common human nature assumed by the Word—particularized by all of the characteristics that any individual instantiation of that nature would have.

The tradition's emphasis on gender and neglect of Jesus' other personal characteristics reveals the distorting influences of implicit bias on christological reflections. Jesus had an eye color, a certain color and texture of hair, and he grew to a certain height. None of those characteristics is considered theologically significant—people with blue or green eyes have not been systematically excluded from the priesthood for failing to appropriately resemble Christ.[92] The fact that Christian patriarchy has singled out one particular characteristic of Jesus for special ontological significance, but not others, indicates that the doctrine of the incarnation is not the source of this problem. If the doctrine were to blame, then groups sharing Jesus' other characteristics would be privileged like men have been privileged in the Christian church.[93] The tradition, however, has had no problem dismissing most of the personal characteristics of Jesus as theologically insignificant. The number of hairs on his head, the color and shape of his eyes, the length of his neck, and the height of his body are all characteristics that Christianity has traditionally ignored. The language he spoke, his spatial reasoning abilities, his mathematical understanding, and his sense of humor have likewise been considered irrelevant to his theological significance. Other characteristics, however, have been prioritized: his maleness, his humanity, and his rationality. Examining the characteristics of the gatekeepers of the tradition reveals a plausible explanation for this inconsistent treatment of Jesus' personal characteristics. All the theologians of the tradition are themselves rational human beings, and the vast majority of them have been male. However, they have had varying amounts hair, different colors of eyes, different heights. They have spoken different languages and had different intellectual gifts and personality traits. Because of the variety of these characteristics within their own primary group of interlocutors, theologians conceded that those characteristics were not essential to the work of the incarnation. But because they were all rational humans, and nearly all men, they emphasized these characteristics as possessing theological significance. The role of implicit biases in these assumptions should be clear. This indicates that androcentric, racially and culturally biased interpretations of the incarnation, rather than the doctrine itself, gives rise to the injustices it has been used to support.

In order to overcome these biases, development of a two-*ousiai* Christology follows the method laid out by feminist theologians for correcting the distortion of implicit androcentric biases that overemphasized the maleness of the incarnation. They responded to androcentric bias by emphasizing a categorical level that is not defined by gender distinctions, in their case turning from the category of male human being to the broader category of generic humanity. Two-*ousiai* Christology does the same thing in a more extreme way. It allows Christians to understand the significance of the incarnation for an even broader category than generic humanity, that of created *ousia*.

3
TRULY CREATED, TRULY CREATOR

The simple claim that all of reality partakes of two *ousiai*, either that of the Creator or that of creation, intervenes helpfully in a number of theological and ethical conversations. It undermines the segregating impulse that would assert that one group of creatures—whether defined by race, gender, culture, or species—is nearer to the divine than others. It opposes the idolatry that would allow certain human beings to take the place of Jesus as the mediator between God and creation, and it does so by positioning human beings in solidarity with all members of creation. Moving beyond that foundational claim in order to develop a preliminary definition of created *ousia* will contribute even more to theological and ethical conversations. Ecomimetic engagement with representatives from a broad spectrum of created beings—from rocks to highly intelligent birds—can shape this definition in ways that intentionally counteract the anthropocentric assumptions that have traditionally shaped christological reflection. This definition of created *ousia* can then be used to reconsider classical understandings of the divine attributes and articulate the coherence of the doctrine of the incarnation.

Feminist critiques of androcentric Christology both undermine discriminatory and idolatrous androcentric interpretations of the incarnation by shifting the focus from the maleness of Jesus to his humanity, *and* reconstruct theological anthropology by including women's lives and experiences as datum for understanding that humanity.[1] Nicaea's two-*ousiai* Christology can similarly undermine discriminatory interpretations of the incarnation while also deepening understandings of creation by shifting the focus from the humanity of Jesus to his creaturely *ousia*. This shift is not quite as straightforward as that performed by feminist theology, however, because those qualities that presumably differentiate human beings from all other creatures have been the focus of much more attention than have the similarities shared by all of creation.[2] Humanity has been a readily understandable category for Ruether's and Johnson's audiences and interlocutors, but created *ousia* is a relatively unexplored concept. Nevertheless, developing a preliminary definition of created *ousia* will demonstrate how Nicaea's two-*ousiai* Christology opposes Christian patriarchy, white supremacy, and ecological degradation while supporting the coherence of the doctrine of the incarnation.[3] Whereas Ruether and Johnson have used women's perspectives and experiences to challenge androcentric assumptions about humanity, an ecomimetic examination of non-human creatures can inform a preliminary understanding of created *ousia*.[4] This definition can then further refine ideas about the other *ousia*, that of the Creator, and how one person could coherently be understood to partake of both *ousiai*.

CREATED *OUSIA*

Just as feminist challenges to the theological significance of Jesus' maleness have not denied his maleness, an emphasis on the importance of the created *ousia* assumed in the incarnation does not deny that Jesus was truly human. There are, however, biological and cosmological reasons to question the usefulness of "human nature" (or any other species-nature) as a category of ultimate significance, whether biological or theological. Both the commonalities across species lines and the differences between individuals within a given species undermine the idea that created natures can be clearly defined. The physical, biological, intellectual, emotional, and moral continuities across species make it difficult, if not impossible, to define a threshold at which something can be said to possess a "rational soul" as opposed to a merely animal one, or an animal soul as opposed to a merely vegetative one. Furthermore, if theological value is based upon one's status as a beloved creation of God, then even the traditional division between animate and inanimate members of creation may not carry the significance that Western thought has traditionally given it.[5] The Christian tradition of creation *ex nihilo* affirms that rocks are created by God just as much as human beings are.

Theology has not completely ignored the characteristics human beings share with other creatures, but it has generally maintained the primacy of human beings even when acknowledging such continuity. Human-as-microcosm soteriological models find commonalities between humans and other creatures across all levels of existence, but they do so by starting with human experience, and assuming that all other material existence is recapitulated in humanity.[6] Emphasizing the divisions within the created world—between mere existence and life, between mere life and feeling, and between feeling and understanding—these approaches ignore the particularity of each member of creation discussed and focus instead only on those characteristics that are shared with human beings.[7] For instance, the abilities of plants to sustain themselves through photosynthesis, a capacity that human beings lack, is ignored in such hierarchies. This is because man-as-microcosm arguments prioritize characteristics and categories that support notions of human superiority. Capacities that human beings lack are therefore ignored as theologically insignificant, while those that are presumed to be unique to human beings are prioritized.[8] An ecomimetic investigation of the commonalities that define created *ousia* cannot start with such privileging of human characteristics. Instead, it will examine a number of different creatures in their own ways of being in order to develop a provisional understanding of created *ousia*. In order to resist implicit and deeply ingrained biases as much as possible, this ecomimetic examination will invert traditional anthropocentric hierarchies by starting with inanimate bodies, then examining the life of a plant, next engaging "irrational" animals, and finally turning to animals that are widely recognized to be "intelligent." Each examination reflects on what the creature in question contributes to an understanding of created *ousia*.

Inanimate Material Bodies

In order to undermine implicit anthropocentric biases, this examination begins with those material bodies considered the furthest removed from human beings—inanimate bodies. Of course, "inanimate" is not a very specific description—the sheer volume of different material bodies that fall into this category is overwhelming. Moving beyond the overgeneralizations that are involved in any system of categorization allows interpreters to recognize the dizzying array of unique bodies that have been unceremoniously lumped together as "other-than-human." Understanding created *ousia* requires close attention to individual material bodies in their particularity. In order to narrow the broad category of inanimate bodies, this inquiry will focus on biological limestone, a particular type of sedimentary rock made up of a substantial amount of calcium carbonate that originates from marine life forms.[9]

Biological limestone forms when deceased plankton, foraminifera, and the fragments of shells are deposited on the sea floor. Once there, time, pressure, and further layers of sediment work together to consolidate them into limestone.[10] This means that biological limestone begins—if it can be said to have a beginning—as a variety of marine life forms, ranging from the simplest plankton to the beautiful shells of more complex creatures. Once formed, this limestone can remain buried for billions of years. It becomes accessible to manipulation once seas have shifted, leaving the limestone buried under newly formed dry land. Once it is exposed, human beings have found such limestone to be a valuable building material. It is soft and malleable when first quarried, but hardens to a durable surface that is resistant to decay upon exposure to the elements.[11] Limestone can be used as building stones, crushed to provide other building materials (including cement and roofing gravel) or to neutralize acid in soil, and can even be used as a filler in products such as animal feed, paint, and paper.[12] As it is heated, crushed, and consumed, it releases both calcium and stored carbon molecules back into the environment.

While buried in its undisturbed environment, limestone functions like a depository of both history and various physical elements. It contains not only calcium and carbon, but many other minerals that have been sequestered for a time from the ongoing exchange of atoms among living things. Its carbon was originally removed from air and sea by the small creatures whose bodies make up the sediment of limestone. Those creatures themselves are part of the complex geophysical process that makes the ocean the largest carbon sink in the world—capturing more of the atmospheric carbon we produce than all the green plants on all the continents combined. Plankton fix carbon during photosynthesis and then either move it up the trophic ladder as transferable energy when the plankton are consumed by larger creatures or carry it to the ocean floor when the plankton die. In the latter case, layers upon layers of such debris sequester that carbon for billions of years as the limestone is formed. By sequestering large amounts of carbon within the earth, limestone plays a part in regulating the climate and keeping the temperatures of the earth within ranges that allow for the flourishing of life. This means that even stones are embedded in the wider web of interrelated material bodies that makes the earth habitable for human beings and other animals. In addition to sequestering carbon, limestone carries tens of millions of years of earth history within its body. Not only is it composed of the atoms that once made up other material bodies, but it preserves the fossils of some of those bodies as well. The only record that remains of many species that evolved and went extinct long before the emergence of humanity is preserved within limestone deposits. Such stones may not have neurons that allow them to categorize and retrieve information, but they nevertheless bear the records of past generations within their bodies.

Human beings have used stones metaphorically to reflect the unchanging, the uncommunicative, the unfeeling, and the unperceiving. Examining the existence of biological limestone without privileging anthropocentric perspectives, however, reveals that it comes into being through the slow accumulation of organic remains. Its unique characteristics are produced by a combination of the bodies out of which it is made, the self-organizing properties of the elements of which it is composed, and the forces of its immediate environment. Over time, these forces can wear it into new shapes as friction and force shave off pieces which are transported to new locales and incorporated into new settings. Although stones do not meet current scientific definitions of life, over a billion years they grow, remain relatively stable for an extended period of time, and then disintegrate with the passage of time. Even stones are engaged in ongoing exchanges with the material bodies that surround them—air, water, other stones, and living bodies such as plants or people. Like living bodies, parts of limestone are taken up into new bodies when they "decompose." Furthermore, although biological limestone might not engage in reflective interpretation of what it has witnessed, it does stand as the only record of times, conditions, and even lifeforms that passed away before the first human beings walked the earth. Setting aside anthropocentric biases that can only call knowledge that which is possessed in the manner of human beings, one might say that these stones possess an embodied kind of ancient knowledge that is inaccessible to more ephemeral creatures.

Based on an examination of biological limestone, created *ousia* might be said to include both elements of stability and principles of change. Athanasius' insight that everything that is created from nothing is susceptible to corruption is supported by contemplating biological limestone—even rocks eventually lose their forms and are changed into something else.[13] But "corruption" may not be the most useful term for this process. That word has a negative connotation, based on the idea that a body's current form and function are proper while any others represent a devolution from its highest and best role. Limestone, however, is born of the "corruption" of marine life and other material bodies, and its own "corruption" funds the growth of artifacts like buildings and roads, as well as that of living bodies like plants and animals. "Transformation" is a better term to describe this process: all bodies that are created from nothing are both transforming in and transformed by their interactions with other bodies. In these ongoing processes of transformation, limestone is interdependent with other parts of creation. Marine life funds its origin, other bodies take up its elements as it disintegrates, and the whole web of life flourishes in an atmosphere that limestone helps to regulate. Far from impassible and unchanging, limestone is characterized by mutuality and mutability, although these characteristics are not easily perceived within the short time span of a human life.

Vegetative Material Bodies

Turning from inanimate objects to the living world, this examination moves to what Aristotle characterized as the lowest tier in the hierarchy of the soul: vegetation. Here the examination must again begin by selecting a particular organism with which to engage. Within the plant kingdom, one finds countless different species with widely varied forms, functions, and existences. Inspired by Jesus' admonition to consider the flowers of the field, this examination focuses on a flowering field grass known as Big Bluestem, or *Andropogon gerardii*.[14] This particular grass is a North American native that, like other plants, derives energy through photosynthetic processes in which water and carbon dioxide are converted into carbohydrates using solar energy and specialized cellular structures. Big Bluestem is a warm-weather perennial that can grow up to ten feet tall, with a main root that descends six to ten feet below the surface.[15] It also produces horizontally growing rhizomes that have helped create the erosion-proof sods of the Midwestern prairies.

Big Bluestem reproduces both vegetatively and sexually; that is, it can produce genetically identical clones via rhizome growth, but it also produces flowers that can cross-pollinate and produce genetically diverse seeds.[16] Sexual reproduction is more prolific after a particularly rainy season, which increases flower and seed production while reducing the likelihood of prairie fires that would destroy new seedlings. However, researchers have found that Big Bluestem generally exhibits a low rate of seed-based reproduction, possibly due to seed predation, the rotting of seeds during damp periods, and the limited space for germination of new plants in crowded prairie ecosystems.[17] Therefore, asexual vegetative regeneration is Big Bluestem's primary mode of propagation. In this process, clones produced from parent rhizomes grow laterally from the parent root system and emerge during the spring as new shoots. These clones can grow and reproduce for many years.[18] In other words, a stand of Big Bluestem that appears from the surface of the earth to be composed of many different plants might be better perceived as one organism. Each stem is genetically identical and connected to a common root system underground. Vegetative regeneration allows Big Bluestem to withstand the regular fires that are part of prairie ecosystems. The underground growth survives even when the aboveground portions of the plant are destroyed, and can therefore regenerate aboveground growth rapidly after fires and other disturbances.

Such clonal regeneration is not unique to Big Bluestem, but it is a property that challenges current understandings of individual material bodies and their lifespans. Although each blade of grass might be perceived as an individual plant, they remain connected to one another in what can also be perceived as a much larger body. Similarly, a particular patch might flourish for one period, while the lifespan of the entire, genetically identical and contiguous body might cover a much longer period of time. Consider, for example, one of the largest and oldest living organisms on earth: a grove of quaking aspens, or *Populus tremuloides*, growing in Fishlake National Forest in Utah.[19] Named "Pando," this grove is composed of approximately 47,000 tree trunks. It covers 107 acres, weighs approximately 6,615 tons, and is estimated to be over 80,000 years old.[20] From a human perspective on the surface of the earth, it appears to be a forest of thousands of individual trees. A subterranean perspective, however, reveals that each tree trunk is a visible part of a larger organism, united to one massive root system. No individual trunk within the forest is 80,000 years old, but the organism itself seems to be. Like Big Bluestem, Pando produces flowers and viable seeds, but its main method of propagation is through vegetative cloning. Long-lived organisms like the quaking aspen make the much shorter lifespans of animals seem insignificant by comparison.

Because of its structure and life cycle, Big Bluestem plays several important roles in its ecosystem. The combination of a deep taproot, shallow rhizomes, and extensive above-ground growth allows this grass to secure soil from erosion by both water and wind.[21] It can access water and other nutrients from much deeper in the soil than can some of its more shallow-rooted neighbors. These other plants benefit both from reduced competition for resources at shallow soil depths and from those resources that Big Bluestem transports to the surface. The aboveground growth provides food to white-tailed deer, bison, and livestock, while the seeds feed a variety of birds. Big Bluestem "suffers" injuries from any number of animals that feed on it, and yet it survives these injuries and continues to produce resources for both itself and other species. Despite the fact that it regenerates most successfully through the budding of underground rhizomes, it continues to expend energy in the production of flowers and seeds that feed the various animals that are part of its ecosystem. The tall, above-ground stems provide physical material for sheltering birds and other small animals throughout the year. Big Bluestem's underground structures make it virtually impervious to fire, and allow it to regenerate quickly after disturbances—thus enabling it to continue providing erosion control, food, and shelter to other species even in the wake of prairie fires. Like the limestone previously examined, Big Bluestem is engaged in ongoing processes of change, including gains and losses to its own particular body. These changes benefit both the grass itself and countless other material bodies.

Although Aristotle believed that the powers of mobility and sensation differentiated animals from plants, plants both sense the environments that surround them and move in response to what they perceive. Evidence indicates that plants sense any number of stimuli, including predation by herbivorous creatures, attacks of soil fungi or microbes, the nutritional quality of soil, and the sufficiency of water supplies. They use these perceptions to govern several "behaviors," including developing new root growth, producing flowers and new shoots, and emitting volatile organic compounds to attract or ward off other creatures.[22] Root growth displays a plant's behavioral response to perception, as the plant "decides" which soil patches to exploit by perceiving nutritional density as well as competition from other plants.[23] This indicates a connection between plant perception and plant mobility. In addition to the faster and more impressive aboveground movements of plants, ranging from the turning of leaves to follow the sun over the course of the day to the dramatic closing of a Venus flytrap, plants also move slowly and deliberately underground through their root growth. The long lifespan of clonal colonies like Big Bluestem and quaking aspens allows this subterranean movement to be displayed above ground as well. Their rhizomal clones extend in one direction or another, in response to the surrounding conditions. As parental structures die off, the body of the organism literally moves from one place to another. It may take tens or hundreds or thousands of years for such movement to become apparent to human observation, but it is occurring. This indicates that the issue is not that Big Bluestem is immobile while human beings are mobile, but that humans move further and more quickly than does prairie grass. Despite Aristotle's assumptions, plants do possess the powers of both sensation and motion.

Plants possess other previously unimagined capacities as well, some that may justify applying the term "intelligence" to plant responses to environmental conditions.[24] From the deployment of chemical responses to predation to the decision to avoid root contact with a neighboring organism, plants display many behaviors that would be called decision-making if they were done by human beings. In addition to the possibility of something analogous to human thought being carried out by individual plants, experiments also indicate that plants communicate with one another to warn neighbors of hostile conditions, like predation. They do so by producing secondary metabolites and using soil fungal networks to facilitate their dissemination to nearby plants.[25] More recently, researchers have found that plants use these fungal networks for more than communication—they can actually share resources as mature plants "feed" younger seedlings.[26] While debate continues over the precise capacities of plant life, it appears that the bright lines that were once thought to separate them from the animal kingdom (perception, mobility, and intelligence) might not be so bright after all.

Challenging assumptions about the limitations of vegetative creatures, this examination reinforces and expands the insights into created *ousia* previously generated. Like the existence of biological limestone, the lives of Big Bluestem and other plants reflect both elements of stability and processes of change. Big Bluestem also undergoes transformation, involving growth, damage, regrowth, and eventual demise over long periods of time. When parts are consumed or shed, or the whole organism passes away, its elements are broken down by animals and microbes and recycled into the larger realm partaking of created *ousia*. Plants like Big Bluestem possess the ability to perceive their surrounding environment and respond accordingly. They also demonstrate a greater degree of freedom than seems to be exercised by biological limestone. They incorporate certain elements from their surrounding environment while avoiding others. Furthermore, the apparent altruism of resource-sharing plants indicates that material bodies are not only related to one another in neutral or self-serving ways. They can materially benefit some creatures, even if they seek to hinder others. The interdependence that characterizes created *ousia* provides the foundation for this kind of reciprocity among material bodies.

"Irrational" Animal Bodies

In Aristotelian hierarchies of being, irrational animals stand between vegetative life and human beings. Insects make up the largest class of organisms found within the animal kingdom, with nine hundred thousand different species identified and estimates that at least that number have yet to be discovered.[27] The order Hymenoptera, which includes ants, wasps, and bees, is one of the four largest orders of insects, with more than seventeen thousand identified species.[28] Within that order, *Atta cephalotes* are leaf-cutter ants that colonize tropical rainforests in Central and South America. As their name suggests, these ants forage for greenery, which they harvest and carry back to their nests. This behavior makes them a significant agricultural pest and therefore has led to their extensive study.

Like many other members of Hymenoptera, *A. cephalotes* are insects that live in large communities governed by a strict caste system in which only the queen produces offspring and the rest of the population cares for the needs of the colony. While an individual worker ant may live for only a few weeks (or as long as a few years), the queen and colony can survive for over a decade.[29] A mature colony is composed of millions of individual ants ranging in size from the quarter-inch length of foraging ants to the two millimeters-long colony dwarfs, and each performs different functions in accordance with their sizes.[30] The foragers travel from the nest to cut large pieces of leaves and petals from plants and bring them back to the colony. There, smaller workers cut the leaf fragments into pieces which even smaller workers mold into building blocks.[31] These ants do not consume the leaves, but rather use these blocks to build a matrix on which they grow a fungus that they do eat.[32] Within their garden, the smallest worker ants tend to the fungus. They keep the garden clean and harvest fungus to feed to the rest of the colony.[33]

Individual ant larva hatch from eggs laid by the queen. Nursery ants care for and feed the larvae until they pupate and begin their adult duties. While one could theoretically observe the life of one such individual ant, the life cycle of *A. cephalotes* can be better understood at the level of the colony (and queen) than of one of the millions of individual worker ants.[34] A mature leaf-cutter queen has one primary task: laying eggs. She carries sperm collected before she established the colony, during her single "nuptial flight," in a specialized spermatheca for the rest of her life. When she lays her eggs, the queen determines whether to "fertilize" an egg (which results in female offspring) or not (which results in males) by opening or shutting the passage connecting this spermatheca to her oviduct.[35] The larvae that hatch from these eggs are fed and cared for by adult worker nurses. Although larval queens are genetically identical to their worker sisters, they grow much larger than the other larvae and pupate into new queens with wings.[36] When a new queen emerges, fully grown, from her pupal stage, she flies from the colony at the beginning of the rainy season and mates with a number of males. Once she has been inseminated, the males die and the queen returns to the ground where she removes her wings and excavates the beginning of a new colony. Once she has dug a small tunnel, she spits out a pellet of fungal strands she carried in her mouth from her birth colony, fertilizes it, and begins laying eggs on the new fungal mat. Within weeks she has raised a generation of worker ants, and the queen retires to her role of egg-laying for her remaining years.[37] The success rate of young queens establishing new colonies is extremely low, with an estimated 90 percent dying before a colony has been founded.[38]

Leaf-cutter ants play a significant role in their ecosystems. A colony can strip vegetation at a prodigious rate, resulting in the death of many of the surrounding plants and the thinning of the forest canopy around the nest.[39] This leads to a reduction in leaf litter and the alteration of the chemical makeup of the soil in the surrounding area. It also results in increasing sunlight and temperature, and decreasing moisture in the area.[40] When a nest is abandoned, the area is quickly recolonized by new vegetation, but the changes caused by the ants alter the makeup of the forest.

Although *A. cephalotes* are highly cooperative within their own colonies, they engage in conflicts with those from outside their home group. When harvesting, sometimes at great distances from the nest, foragers use their antennae to scan ants they encounter on their trips to and from the plants. Each ant carries a "home scent" that allows their colonymates to recognize one another in these encounters. However, the foragers will immediately attack any foreign ants that do not carry that scent.[41] The largest of the colony ants function as soldiers, armed with sharp mandibles that can dismember enemy insects.[42] These giants defend the nest from large invaders, while smaller workers play a different role in colony defense. The smaller ants have been seen hitchhiking on large leaf fragments the foragers are carrying back to the nest. Studies suggest that they may provide the foragers with defense from parasitic flies, or that they may be cleaning the leaves prior to their entry into the nest to defend against fungal pathogens.[43] In either case, not only the giant soldiers, but even the smallest ants protect the wellbeing of the entire colony.

Leaf-cutter ants challenge many of our presuppositions about "irrational" animal life. Because of their symbiotic relationship with the fungus they consume, leaf-cutter ants are farming organisms—a behavior rarely seen outside of human beings. Their symbiotic relationship with the fungus has altered the genetic makeup of the ants—*A. cephalotes* show decreased numbers and different types of genes involved in nutrient acquisition compared to other ants.[44] Viewing this relationship from an animal-centric perspective, it can be said that *A. cephalotes* have developed the ability to "digest leaves," by domesticating and transporting the fungus to their new colonies. From a fungal-centric perspective, however, one could just as accurately say that the fungus has developed the ability to forage for leaves and migrate from one subterranean location to another by domesticating ants.[45] From either perspective, the deep interdependence of these two material bodies is obvious. In addition to their mutualistic relationship with the fungus, *A. cephalotes* also challenge our presuppositions about what makes an individual organism an individual. Like the relationship between individual shoots of a Big Bluestem clonal colony, the ants of an *A. cephalotes* colony might be perceived as either millions of individual organisms, or parts of one larger organism. Individual ants treat their colony mates as a kind of extended self while differentiating them from the distinctively "other" ants of foreign colonies. Thus, the functioning colony can be fruitfully understood as a superorganism, in which the brain is the whole society at work, and the superorganism's evolutionary success is determined by whether it produces new queens who establish new colonies.[46]

Like biological limestone and Big Bluestem grass, *A. cephalotes* undermine anthropocentric assumptions and contribute to an understanding of created *ousia*. These ants both perceive the world around them and communicate with one another. They are deeply interdependent with other species: the colony grows through a complex metabolic pathway that includes leaf and fungus as well as ant biology. Like the inanimate limestone and the living Big Bluestem already examined, *A. cephalotes* experience both the transience of their short individual lifespans and a degree of stability in the longer life cycle of their colonies. Like other material bodies, the way that they live shapes their surrounding environment. They participate in the ongoing cycles of transformation, growth, and death that seem to characterize all of created reality.

"Rational" Animals

The final distinction in Aristotle's categories is between bodies that possess animal souls and those that possess rational souls. He assumed that while all animals possessed the abilities to perceive and move about, human beings were the only material bodies that possessed intelligence, including the powers of thought and reflection. Throughout history human beings have claimed that we have certain intellectual capacities that are not shared with any other species, evidenced by such things as our use of tools and our capacity for language. In recent decades, studies of animal cognition have challenged the uniqueness of many of these capacities, suggesting that while we are better than other animals at any number of cognitive tasks, there may not be a qualitative divide between our abilities and those of other animals. Further, it seems that there are many cognitive tasks that different animals perform better than human beings.[47] These capacities exist not only in primates like ourselves, but also in elephants, birds, and even the invertebrate octopus. In order to resist anthropomorphic projection, this examination will avoid intelligent mammals and instead focus on a species of birds from the corvid family, which includes ravens, crows, and jays. More specifically, it takes up the western scrub-jay, or *Aphelocoma californica*.

Western scrub-jays are small, non-migratory birds.[48] They are found from southern Canada to Central Mexico, and their diet varies by season. In the spring and summer they live on fruit and small animals ranging from insects to young birds of other species, while in the winter they switch to berries, nuts, grains, and seeds.[49] Although young scrub-jays learn to fly and leave the nest at about eighteen days of age, they remain with their parents until they are five months old. Scrub-jays reach sexual maturity within a year, but males need to establish (and be able to defend) a territory before they mate—a job that can take several years.[50] Once the male has established his territory, he builds a nest in the spring and begins trying to attract a mate. Once he is successful, the pair will remain together for the rest of their lives.[51] After mating, the female scrub-jay lays one to six eggs. The eggs hatch in approximately eighteen days, and the female stays with the chicks while the male forages for food.[52] Western scrub-jays are vulnerable to predation from many different animals, including snakes, raccoons, skunks, and other corvids, but if they escape such predation they can live up to fifteen years.[53] They are known to engage in mourning behavior when they encounter the body of a dead scrub-jay, crying by the body for a half hour and remaining near it for days.[54]

Like other corvids, western scrub-jays collect and cache seeds during the summer and fall for future use. Although they retrieve most of their stores, the seeds that they do not recover sprout—making these birds an important seed-dispersal vector in the life cycles of many plants.[55] Western scrub-jays also form a mutualistic relationship with Columbian black-tailed deer, eating small parasites off of their skin.[56] In addition to these beneficial functions within their ecosystem, scrub-jays can become agricultural pests, particularly due to their preference for certain fruit trees.[57] They are both predator and prey, killing and eating animals ranging from moth larvae to small birds and lizards, while also serving as prey to larger carnivores.

Corvids' impressive cognitive abilities have made them the subject of a great deal of study. Many corvids store food for the winter in hundreds of hiding places, are able recall the locations of their caches months later, and retrieve the food at need. Study of western scrub-jay caching has led researchers to hypothesize that these little birds possess several cognitive capacities that were once believed to belong to human beings alone. One example of this has to do with episodic memory, or the ability to recall not only *that* something occurred (the seeds were hidden) or *where* it occurred (in that cache), but *when*, or how long ago it happened. When scrub-jays in the lab were taught that their preferred food (wax-moth larvae, or wax worms) spoiled after a few days, they abandoned the wax worm caches if they were prevented from returning for forty-eight hours.[58] They could remember how long it had been since they had hidden the food and abandoned perishable food that had passed its "expiration date."

In addition to having a temporal element to their memories, researchers have also argued that western scrub-jays are capable of mental attribution, or the ability to understand what other birds can perceive and what they may do with their observations. Western scrub-jays are notorious thieves. They will watch other birds hiding food and then raid those caches once they are unwatched. Studies have revealed that scrub-jay caching behavior changes in the presence of other scrub-jays—they attempt to hide their food out of sight of other birds, and if that is not possible, they engage in a process of re-caching, moving the food several times.[59] More interestingly, birds that have never raided another bird's cache themselves ("naïve jays") do not exhibit the same re-caching behavior, indicating that the suspicious jays are projecting their own past thievery onto the watching birds.[60] Further research indicates that scrub-jays are even able to reflect on their own knowledge, something called metacognition. When allowed to watch two food-hiding events simultaneously, one of which would require closer attention for them to be able to re-locate the cache if they were given the chance to raid it, the birds allocate their mental and observational capacities accordingly.[61] Western scrub-jays display an array of cognitive abilities that were once considered unique to human beings.

Examination of western scrub-jays reinforces the preliminary definition of created *ousia* developed in conversation with rocks, plants, and insects, while challenging anthropocentric assumptions about human superiority. Western scrub-jays are in interdependent relationships with the other material bodies that surround them. They come into being, grow, and mature while consuming other creatures, and they are in turn consumed by other creatures. They contribute to the well-being of others within their ecosystems, from providing deer with pest control to serving as seed-dispersers for a variety of plants. Like *A. cephalotes* and Big Bluestem, scrub-jays are capable of perceiving the world around them, and they use those perceptions to modify their own behavior. They experience both stability and change, they engage in ongoing processes of transformation, and their bodies incorporate the material conditions they have experienced—all things they share with other creatures partaking of created *ousia*.

The cognitive capacities of Western scrub-jays challenge anthropocentric assumptions about the uniqueness of human capacities while further reinforcing the theological gains of Nicaea's two-*ousiai* Christology. In line with Nicene logic, Christian theologians have long held that a qualitative divide separates human beings from the Creator.[62] Anthropocentric biases, however, have often led human beings to assume that there is a qualitative divide that separates human beings from all other members of creation as well. This supposed qualitative divide is most often associated with rationality—a trait that was once used to support patriarchal hierarchies that dismissed women as sub-rational as well. The anthropocentric biases that still influence scientific investigations lead to an unreasonable resistance to calling capacities such as those exhibited by the Western scrub-jay "intelligence." Instead, many would argue, that term should be reserved to human beings alone and "cognition" would suffice to describe animal mental processes.

These biases can be seen in those who cannot accept that some animals display skills once thought to belong to humans alone. For example, upon the report that Western scrub-jays engaged in mental attribution, some scientists felt the need to rebut the finding.[63] Although not working with the birds themselves, these researchers designed a computer simulation to demonstrate that stress might explain the scrub-jays' re-caching behavior. In turn, the original researchers designed new experiments, carried out with actual living birds, that ruled out the stress theory.[64] The fact that scrub-jays appear to possess episodic memories and the capacity for mental attribution, capacities once thought to be unique to human beings, as well as spatial recall that far exceeds that of human beings, calls into question the idea that human intelligence is qualitatively different from that of other animals. Cross-species continuity of intelligence makes sense from a scientific perspective. Evolution explains that all material bodies share a common history, although each is shaped by a combination of universal forces and the particular local communities of material bodies with whom they interact. Human beings *should* share traits with other material bodies, although the precise combinations of those traits vary from species to species. This goes for cognitive abilities as well as physical traits.[65] The term "intelligence" should not be relegated to only one particular set of cognitive abilities. It is more scientifically fruitful to consider the multiple kinds of intelligence possessed by a wide variety of beings. Instead of asking *whether* western scrub-jays are intelligent, it is important to pay attention to *how* their particular forms of intelligence enable them to function within their environments. There is much to learn about the intelligence of an *A. cephalotes* colony or a patch of Big Bluestem, if the anthropocentric biases that insist on the impossibility of intelligence among any "lower" lifeforms can be overcome.

Created Ousia: *A Preliminary Definition*

Traditional formulations of conciliar Christology have focused on the Word's assumption of humanity, identified by those characteristics understood to be essential to human nature. These include such attributes as peccability, contingency, perceptibility, mutability, and limitations (in power, time, and space). Focusing instead on the Word's assumption of created *ousia* illuminates the shared nature of these attributes. To be created means to be caught up in ongoing processes of transformation, in which one both alters other creatures, and is in turn transformed by them as well.[66] All creatures are subject to transformation—what Athanasius called corruption, but what process theologians refer to as "becoming." To be created does not mean to be fully formed and then placed within the universe. Instead, it means to be called into being within the universe and to be subject to the forces that govern that universe. To be created means to be sustained by elements of stability that prevent annihilation, but it also means being subject to the transforming creativity that empowers this process of becoming. It means being dependent on some creatures while supporting others. In other words, it means being part of an interdependent community that shapes its individual members even as it is shaped by them.

This ongoing process of transformation does not result in uniformity among creatures. Rather, it contributes to the differences that make each species and each individual member of each species unique. The particular socio-ecological communities in which each body is located allows its capacities to develop in different ways. Being a particularly located material body with its own particular genetic and individual history enables a patch of Big Bluestem to derive the energy it needs to live and grow directly from sunlight—a capacity that human beings have never possessed. In contrast, the energy needed to form biological limestone comes from the weight of accumulated sediment—a pressure that would kill most living creatures. Leaf-cutter ants and western scrub-jays, like other animals, derive their energy from the consumption of other living (or recently living) creatures. The processes of transformation to which all creation is subject enable millions of ants to function with one purpose, even as they carry out separate tasks, while also equipping western scrub-jays to negotiate complex relationships with pilfering relatives. These processes enable Big Bluestem to provide both food and shelter to a host of other living creatures without jeopardizing the grass' own survival. Viewing the ability to transform and be transformed as inherent in created *ousia* means that plurality, not only of bodies but also of the characteristics and capacities that those bodies possess, is inherent within creation.

The fact that all material bodies are interrelated with one another indicates that the interests of no single species—not even human beings—can be isolated from those of others. The human body is itself composed of trillions of other material bodies. In turn, it also plays roles in larger material bodies. Plant clonal colonies like Big Bluestem challenge the idea that organisms that appear to be separate individuals can so easily be categorized as different material bodies. Social insects like the leaf-cutter ant take this challenge even further, suggesting that organisms that exist in separate bodies moving independently of one another might still be better understood as parts of a larger organism. What science, law, and theology recognize as an individual human being can be fruitfully understood as a community teeming with millions of different species of living creatures. The ecosystem of the human body can also be viewed as one part of an even larger organism. Just as individual bodies evolve within an environment, bodies and environments together "evolve as a single, self-regulating system," and the entire planet Earth can, from this perspective, be understood as a superorganism that regulates itself through the material bodies of which it is composed.[67] All material bodies, it seems, are composed of smaller material bodies, and in turn function as parts in ever larger material bodies.[68]

Created *ousia* is characterized by mutual transformation and interrelation. This preliminary definition of created *ousia* contributes to the theological insights of Nicene two-*ousiai* logic in three ways. First, it provides content to the claim that all of creation shares in *something* that crosses species boundaries.[69] Created *ousia* enables and ensures that everything engages in interrelated processes of mutual transformation. Our bodies are made up of different species, and our communities incorporate plants, animals, and inanimate bodies as well as other human beings. We cannot be removed from this web of interdependence and still function any more than our brains can be removed from our bodies and still function. This web of interdependence with all material bodies better explains how something entering creation at one point could be shared across the full breadth of created *ousia* than does the more nominal category of human nature.[70] This indicates that created *ousia* can affirm the universal reach of the incarnation in ways that focusing on the particularity of Christ's human nature cannot.

Second, although all of creation partakes of the same created *ousia*, this preliminary definition explains the wide variety of forms that created *ousia* actually takes. Creation is not uniform, but the interdependence and mutability that all created bodies share is what leads to their different expressions of this shared *ousia*. Creatures develop their capacities in response to the socio-ecological systems in which they find themselves. Their ecology—that is, the other created bodies that surround and even overlap their own—is key.

Third, individual species are defined by their unique combinations of characteristics and capacities. Although some of these characteristics and capacities do overlap species' boundaries, "higher" species do not possess all of the characteristics that "lower" species possess plus some unique traits of their own. It is not true that animals have all of the capacities that plants do, plus some additional traits that place them higher on the Great Chain of Being (e.g., animals certainly lack the ability to photosynthesize). Nor is it true that human beings possess all of the capacities that "lower" animals do, plus some additional ones that place them even higher (on a physiological level, we lack the gift of flight, and on a cognitive level, we certainly do not have the spatial recall of a western scrub-jay). This is why the human-as-microcosm argument is ultimately an insufficient guarantor that whatever benefits the Word conveys in the incarnation could be passed on to the rest of the cosmos by means of its assumption of a particularly human nature. Human nature does not encapsulate all of the different forms of existence that material bodies experience.

Furthermore, whatever theological claims are bound up in the predicates traditionally ascribed to humanity are not jeopardized by focusing on the created *ousia*, rather than the human nature, of the incarnation. Individual instantiations of created *ousia* are characterized by the same attributes traditionally attached to individual human beings.[71] Individual creatures are mutable, passible, and temporally and spatially limited. If they are living, then they are mortal. Even if they are not living, they will eventually disintegrate and be taken up into new creatures. Shifting the emphasis from human nature to created *ousia* allows Christians to affirm the same characteristics of created entities without privileging any one species or any single group within a species. This definition of created *ousia*, therefore, provides a foundation for eco-liberative resistance to Christian patriarchy, white supremacy, and anthropocentric exploitation of the natural world.

DIVINE ATTRIBUTES

The ecomimetic examination of different kinds of material bodies indicates that there are many other ways of being than those experienced by humans, other ways of perceiving the world and processing the information provided by it, and other manners of interacting with different beings. Similarly, it implies that one of these is not necessarily higher or better than another. This challenges *a priori* approaches to naming the divine attributes that are shaped by assumptions both originating from and reinforcing an anthropomorphic portrait of the divine.

Whereas theological perspectives from the third and fourth centuries were instrumental in setting the terms for future christological debates, the debates of medieval theologians over how to properly describe God sharpened classical theism's portrait of the divine. Drawing on Aristotle's work, theologians of this period adapted ideas of God as the unmoved mover in order to demonstrate the existence of God based on natural human reason rather than scriptural revelation.[72] In order to do so, they had to address whether human beings were capable of having natural knowledge of God at all, and if so, what kind of knowledge they might possess.

Answers to these questions attempted to bridge the chasm between apophatic theology, which denies that finite creatures are capable of forming accurate concepts of God, and cataphatic theology, which allows that human beings are capable of some—albeit limited—understandings of God. The *via negativa* that has come to be associated with Pseudo-Dionysius, a Christian mystic from the early sixth century, denies the literal applicability of *any* language to the divine.[73] Beginning with the names that Scripture provides for God, Pseudo-Dionysius first affirms that they are true names of God, and then he denies their literal applicability to the divine.[74] The complex procedure of such apophaticism must both affirm and deny the applicability of all language to the divine, while somehow resolving the tension between that affirmation and denial.[75] Consider the attribute of "just," for example: in order to pay adequate linguistic attention to divine transcendence, theologians would have to affirm that God is just, deny that by saying that God is not just, and then negate the contradiction between the two. According to this approach, the only thing that can simply be denied of God, without simultaneously affirming it and negating the contradiction, is whatever is evil.[76] If theology instead denies only some creaturely attributes to the divine, it can easily succumb to the illusion that language is capable of conveying positive knowledge of God.[77]

Although many later theologians found Pseudo-Dionysius' dedication to the preservation of divine transcendence persuasive, they nevertheless needed to affirm that human beings could have *some* true knowledge of God, or else the entire project of theology would seem to fail. They therefore distinguished between natural knowledge of God—that which is available to human reason from observation of the natural world—and supernatural knowledge of God—that which is available only through God's self-disclosure.[78] They agreed that human reason could not arrive at such theological doctrines as the Trinity or the incarnation without divine revelation, but argued that other concepts, such as the existence of God and some attributes that should be affirmed of God, could be deduced from experience with the natural world.[79] Both kinds of knowledge, however, indicated a departure from Pseudo-Dionysius' radically apophatic approach, because both allowed that human beings could possess adequate concepts about the divine, whether they arrived at those concepts through revelation or human reason.

Anselm of Canterbury provides an early and illustrative example of these efforts. As he explained in the preface to the *Proslogium*, Anselm sought a logical proof of God's existence that did not rely on Scripture, but was rather based on reason alone.[80] Without delving into all of the details of his argument, his conclusion that God is "that than which nothing greater can be thought," and indeed, "better than can be thought," provided the foundation for attributing to God all of those characteristics that it is better to possess than not to possess.[81]

The greatness of these attributes is assumed to be self-evident: obviously it is greater to be impassible than to be passible, greater to be living than to be nonliving, and greater to be unbounded than to be bounded. The problem with this argument is that any list of great-making attributes reflects a wish list of the characteristics that the person making the list values. Those constructing such lists assume that it is universally recognized that these characteristics are better to possess than not to possess. If people do not realize that it is better to be immutable than to be mutable, there is something deficient in their reasoning. In 2013 marketers for AT&T U-verse cashed in on the emotional force of such arguments with their ad campaign featuring the tagline, "It's not complicated." In these ads, an adult asked a group of children simply formed value judgment questions, like "What is better, faster or slower?" and other questions about being bigger, and having more.[82] In unison the children opted for the "great-making characteristic"—faster, bigger, more. Since even children know which is better, these commercials imply, you would have to be a bit simple to question these values. The problem with both the commercials and the Anselmian divine attributes is that what makes having a characteristic greater than not having it is contextual. While faster, bigger, and more coverage are valuable characteristics for a wireless network, they are not universally great. Great barbecue requires slow cooking, nanotechnology reflects the value of the small, and more salt does not always help the flavor of a meal or the health of those eating it. Whether it is better to be immutable or changing depends upon the perspective of the individual, and no human being has the perspective of the divine. Lists of divine attributes reflect the values of those making such lists.[83] Since the *a priori* divine attributes were developed by human beings who were usually empowered human men, they reflect anthropocentric, and in many cases androcentric, preferences.

This can be seen in the case of two such great-making characteristics—immutability and omnipotence. Human beings are subject to change caused by forces beyond our control. For a variety of reasons, philosophers and theologians have historically tended to write from a perspective of privilege, and from this perspective change usually entails diminishment. Those who view change in this way would view imperviousness to change as an attribute that it is better to possess than not to possess. Similarly, privileged people characteristically attach a high value to power, defined in an active way as the ability to bring about whatever state of affairs one wishes to bring about.[84] In contrast, there are great numbers of people who live under oppression and who therefore view change and power in a different light. For people in these conditions, change represents their only hope for improvement in their circumstances. Furthermore, their oppression stems from the disproportionate exercise of power by others, an exercise which impairs their own powers of self-determination. From this perspective, defining omnipotence as the determination of everything that happens ties it too closely to the foundation of their oppression. For those suffering oppression, creative possibilities are greater than immutability, and shared power is greater than omnipotence. Oppressors and beneficiaries of oppression generally want the status quo to remain indefinitely and therefore value immutability highly, while the oppressed want the current state of affairs overturned and thus value the changeability necessary for acts of creative liberation. Understandings of the divine advanced by those marginalized by society have different emphases than those supported by the dominant tradition. This is not to argue that mutability or sharing of power are necessarily better descriptions of the divine being than are immutability and omnipotence. Rather it is meant to point out the ways in which implicit biases rooted in individual contexts shape which characteristics are considered great-making and which are not.

Although scholastic theologians did not indicate an awareness of the contextual biases that might have shaped their conclusions about what characteristics are universally "great," they did agree that human beings do not possess the perspective of the divine. Creation *ex nihilo* carries with it two distinct but related insights on this point. The first is that there is an ontological divide between God and everything that God creates. For this reason, even if creaturely concepts could be used to describe God, a distinction between the way they are applied to creatures and the way they are applied to God has to be maintained. The second insight is that God causes everything that exists. Therefore, whatever characteristics creatures possess find their origin in God. For these reasons Thomas Aquinas denied that concepts used to describe both creatures and the Creator were used either univocally (implying there was no qualitative distinction between the two) or equivocally (implying the two were unrelated). Such language, Aquinas taught, was used analogically instead.[85] Aquinas used analogical predication to describe how positive names, like loving or just, can be applied to both creatures and God. Although the concepts described by the words apply most properly to God as the Creator and origin of all creaturely characteristics, our understanding of the terms applies in a different way to creatures.[86] In other words, how human beings understand "just" is derived from observations of justice in the created world, and therefore what the term signifies in our mind properly applies to created reality. Aquinas understood this justice to be related to, but distinct from, divine justice, which is the principle and cause of all creaturely forms of justice.[87] Aquinas understood "negative names" of God differently. Divine attributes that are not also attributed to creatures but stand rather as denials of the creaturely condition, like omnipotence or immutability, signified the distinction between God and creation.[88]

The Franciscan theologian Duns Scotus vehemently disagreed with Aquinas, arguing that there was no middle ground between univocal and equivocal applications of concepts and terms.[89] Either the concept is univocal and to affirm and deny it of the same thing results in a contradiction, or it is equivocal because the meanings differ.[90] The point on which Scotus disagrees implicitly with Aquinas, and directly with Henry of Ghent, is not whether terms might apply differently to God and to creatures—he allows that they do.[91] Scotus' objection was that this difference indicates a complexity inherent in what Aquinas calls analogy that does not serve Scotus' search for a simple concept that can be applied to both God and creatures.[92] Even when Scotus identifies the simple concept "being" as one that can be applied univocally to both God and creatures, he also introduces a modal distinction between infinite and finite being that preserves a distinction between the two.[93] Thus, while a transcendental such as "wise" might be applied to both God and to a person, Scotus allows that God is infinitely wise while a person can only be wise in a finite way.[94] Whether Scotus succeeds in preserving his particular definition of univocal or defeating Aquinas' understanding of analogy is outside the scope of the current argument. The point is that the tradition recognizes that there is a distinction between the ways that terms can describe God and the ways that the same terms can describe creatures.

Traditional notions of divinity include some predications that are applied to both creatures and the Creator—albeit with a modal or analogical distinction—and other predications that are the denial of creaturely attributes. For example, Anselm asserts that the being who is greater than can be thought is just, truthful, happy, percipient, omnipotent, merciful, impassible, living, wise, good, eternal, and unbounded.[95] Many of these attributes (just, truthful, happy, percipient, merciful, living, wise, and good) are positive names that can also be applied to creatures, while others (omnipotent, impassible, eternal, and unbounded) are negations of properties inherent in created *ousia*.[96] Although the latter set of attributes seem to be upholding divine transcendence through apophatic denials of creaturely limitations, these apparently apophatic attributes have functioned cataphatically in coherence debates, asserting positive claims about the divine nature that are in turn used to attack the coherence of the incarnation.

The selectivity of denial exhibited by classical theism—which does not deny assertions that God is loving or spirit or truthful—implies that both the cataphatic and the apophatic descriptors used convey positive content about the divine. This selectivity once again reveals the anthropocentric biases involved in these debates. Although classical theism does not explicitly call the created condition evil, perhaps because of the Christian affirmation of creation as "good," it does treat many characteristics of creaturely existence as if they are "evil" and therefore inappropriate for naming the divine. This can be seen particularly in the failure of classical theism to negate seemingly apophatic claims that God is not mortal, mutable, passible, or located in time or space.[97] Anthropocentric assumptions govern this determination of the "goodness" of certain created characteristics (such as being just, happy, living) and the "evilness" of others (such as mutability, finitude, and interdependence or limitation in power). In order properly to preserve divine transcendence while avoiding anthropocentric distortions, all of those attributes that characterize God's good creation—including mutability, passibility, and dependence—should also be used to name God (although they should also be denied, and the contradiction between the naming and the denial be negated).

In order to avoid anthropocentric distortions, Christians should not assume that the human preferences reflected in classical theism's lists of divine attributes necessarily disclose the divine essence. God's transcendence of creation makes it impossible for creatures on this side of the ontological divide to form a fully comprehensive concept of the divine nature.[98] However, this does not foreclose theology from saying anything at all about God. If God is the Creator of all that exists, as Christians claim, it is safe to assume that creation reveals *something* about God even if it does not provide either knowledge or comprehension of the divine *ousia*. The way that the tradition has most successfully described this relationship of creation to knowledge about the divine is through causal relationships. As Aquinas explains, the created intellect knows through sensible things, and through these things it can know God's "relationship with creatures so far as to be the cause of them all; also that creatures differ from him, inasmuch as he is not in any way part of what is caused by him; and that creatures are not removed from him by reason of any defect on his part, but because he superexceeds them all."[99] Of course, Christian claims about God's relationship to creation are not restricted to causality. Scripture provides a number of descriptions of God's estimation of and relationship to creation.

What one values and what one cares for reveals information about the individual doing the valuing and caring, even if it cannot explain the essence of that individual. Scriptural claims about God's relationship to creation indicate that God considers creation "good" (Gen 1:4, 10, 12, 18, 21, 25, 31), cares for the well-being of individual parts of creation (Ps 104; Job 38–41; Matt 6:25-30, 10:29), and loves the whole of creation (John 3:16). Based on these claims—that God loves, cares for, and considers good all that God creates—an understanding of created *ousia* reveals something about *what God values*, even though it *cannot define what God is*. Created *ousia* is mutable, transient, diverse, and interdependent—all characteristics that have been devalued by classical descriptions of divine great-making attributes.

Each material body is constantly engaged in processes of transformation as it grows, maintains itself, and eventually diminishes or dies. If God finds this world of shifting landmasses, variable weather, metabolic processes, emerging species, and changing landscapes "good," then it would seem to follow that God values change. Since there is nothing in this world that is immutable, calling immutability a great-making attribute seems like a repudiation of the goodness of creation. Without change, there is no birth, growth, or life. Although human beings who perceive mutability as a threat to security might view such changeability as a defect, this negative valuation does not necessarily reflect the divine view of mutability. If every created material body is, and always has been, mutable, it seems more likely that God views mutability favorably. Indeed, this is a fundamental tenet of process theology, which privileges "becoming" over "being."[100] God does not seem to devalue created beings for undergoing change.

The inference that God values transient beings follows from the conclusion that God values mutable creatures, and Scripture affirms this as well (see especially Eccl 3:1-8). Because everything is eventually transformed, if God cares about individual material bodies at all, then God values transient beings. As the author of Matthew notes, God's providence extends to birds that are sold two for a penny, and to weeds that are thrown into the oven for fuel (6:25-30, 10:29). Whether they exist for moments or for millennia, all material bodies pass away. According to Christian doctrine, God cares for them all. Although human beings tend to disparage things that are shorter-lived—consider the "insignificance" of a mayfly—there is nothing to indicate that the duration of a thing's existence reflects the amount that God cares for it. Human beings have viewed mortality and transience as defects rather than as elements of created goodness, but God's valuing of creation does not follow human priorities.[101] From an anthropocentric perspective, God values mortal creatures *in spite of* their mortality. But from another perspective, one might say that God also values the transience of created bodies; their very mortality might be part of what makes them good.

The great variety of material bodies that makes up creation indicates that God also values diversity. The processes of transformation in which all material bodies are involved have led to a dizzying array of different kinds of bodies. There is not just one species, or one living creature, or one animal, any more than there is just one planet, or one solar system, or one galaxy. Creation is marked by plurality. If God considers this planet, with its land and water, mountains and valleys, sea creatures and land animals, to be good, then God values and cares for the flourishing of a multiplicity of created bodies.[102]

Finally, God values creaturely interdependence. All of creation is mutually related, coming into being from other material bodies and passing away into other material bodies.[103] Nothing exists in solitary independence. Water shapes stones that in turn change the composition of the water. Plants transform molecules in the soil and atmosphere into carbohydrates, which fuel the rest of life on this planet. Bacteria transform multicellular organisms back into molecules in the soil, water, and atmosphere once they have died. Mountains rise up with the shifting of tectonic plates, and are worn back down by the forces of wind and rain. What are perceived as individual creatures are often complex ecosystems teeming with different material bodies, all exchanging their products with one another. Interdependence lies at the heart of this created order, indicating that God values this kind of interrelatedness. It would seem that God does not find passibility, mutability, mortality, or other forms of transience to be defects detracting from the value of creation.

Although this does not rule out the possibility that the divine *ousia* is impassible, simple, immutable, and immortal, it provides no support for *a priori* assumptions that a being should (let alone must) be any of these things in order to be divine.[104] Observation of the created order cannot render an adequate literal description of the divine *ousia* because the idea of divine transcendence forecloses all such literal descriptions.[105] This transcendence undermines all attempts to name the divine using concepts derived from finite creaturely existence.[106] In line with the apophatic impulses of Christian tradition, this ecomimetic interpretation does not try to describe the divine essence. Instead, it challenges the deference given to descriptions that have dominated classical theism for centuries. Without claiming that God is mutable, mortal, or dependent, recognizing that these conditions characterize all of creation undermines descriptions of God that deny the value of these characteristics.

The ecomimetic investigation of created *ousia* does provide *a posteriori* support for at least one attribute attached to divine *ousia*. All material bodies are involved in continual processes of mutual transformation, but they also experience stability and continuity. Big Bluestem, leaf-cutter colonies, western scrub-jays and human beings flourish for a time before passing away. Limestone persists at the bottom of the ocean for a much longer period of time, before it is eventually taken up into other bodies. Similarly, all material bodies are subject to physical forces beyond their control, but these constants that govern the universe do not change. These physical facts resonate with the theological notion that all of creation comes from nothing and would return to nothing but for the divine will. From a material perspective, however, we know that nothing that exists genuinely ceases to be. Rather it is always transformed into something else. The stability that allows material bodies to exist, the constants that govern the universe, and the persistence of matter beyond the lifetimes of the creatures it composes all provide support for attributing to the divine an unchanging faithfulness that enables all of creation to exist.

COHERENCE DEBATES

Because created *ousia* can be described with the same terms traditionally ascribed to the human nature, recovering a two-*ousiai* understanding of the incarnation does not itself resolve all debates over the coherence of the incarnation. It does, however, provide grounds for reconsidering how certain divine attributes are understood and for understanding created *ousia* in ways that transcend classical definitions of human nature.

Divine faithfulness is not a characteristic that critics point to as creating incoherence in the doctrine of the incarnation. Rather, they argue that things like divine invisibility, immutability, and inability to die are logically incompatible with human visibility, changeability, and mortality.[107] Anselm himself provides a response to the first contradiction between divine invisibility and human visibility. He did not end his theological reflection with the argument that God is that than which nothing greater can be thought. Further in the *Proslogion*, he concludes that God is "something greater than can be thought."[108] Anselm thus denies that our intellects can grasp the truth about God. This incapacity affects the way we describe God as well. For Anselm God is invisible because of a human inability to properly see, which comes from our "own darkness," rather than from an attribute of divine invisibility.[109] Similarly, our inability to hear, smell, taste, and touch God stems from the fact that the senses of our souls "have been stiffened, dulled, and obstructed by the longstanding weakness of sin."[110] Based on this argument, the attribute of invisibility is better understood as expressing the inability of created beings to comprehend the divine nature than as a positive attribute of that nature. Although the tradition's commitment to divine incorporeality has generally taken divine invisibility to mean more than the human incapacity to see God, Anselm's argument does provide an avenue for remaining agnostic about whether or not God is actually (i.e. univocally) invisible.

Even if God is literally invisible, this need not contradict assertions that in Jesus the Word was visible. Consideration of ordinary human beings demonstrates that even a regular created being can be both visible and invisible at the same time. No one would deny that human beings are visible. There are, however, many things about human beings that are not. Those who affirm the existence of immaterial souls hold that they are invisible. Human thoughts and emotions are similarly invisible. A person's humanity would more likely be called into question if they lacked the ability to think or feel than if they became invisible. Therefore, without even considering the unique situation of the incarnation, it is logically coherent to claim that one person can be both visible and invisible at the same time.

Immutability creates another kind of difficulty. Classical theism defines divine immutability as being entirely unchanging. Aquinas holds that the most perfect being is the one that is entirely actualized, containing nothing that is merely potential.[111] If a being changes, it must be for the better or for the worse. If God could change for the better, then God would not be perfect before that change; and if God could change for the worse, then God would not be perfect after that change. In order for God to be completely actualized, then God cannot be capable of becoming anything more or less than God already is. This "strong" definition of divine immutability runs into trouble with scriptures that impute a variety of changes to God.[112] In response to the strong definition of immutability, Stephen Davis argues that divine immutability does not require a strict unchangeableness, but rather is "designed to preserve the view that God is faithful in keeping his promises, that his basic benevolent nature remains the same; that he is not fickle and capricious and can be relied upon."[113] Davis concedes that this assurance does require *a kind of changelessness* in "God's basic nature and faithfulness to his promises," but denies that it requires a notion of God's being entirely unchanging in all other senses.[114] Davis' version of divine immutability has come to be called the "weak" view, as opposed to the "strong" view that insists that God is absolutely unchanging in any way.[115]

This weak view of immutability, however, does not resolve the apparent incoherence of conciliar Christology. The Council of Nicaea anathematized "those who say 'there once was when he was not', and 'before he was begotten he was not', and that he came to be from things that were not, or from another hypostasis or substance, affirming that the Son of God is subject to change or alteration."[116] That council does not apply immutability to the Son's faithfulness in accordance with the weak view. Instead, it actually alleges something unchanging about his nature. As further evidence of this intention, Pawl offers two of Cyril's letters that were approved by later councils.[117] In his "Third Letter to Nestorius," Cyril argues,

> He did not cast aside what he was, but although he assumed flesh and blood, he remained what he was, God in nature and truth. We do not say that his

flesh was turned into the nature of the godhead or that the unspeakable Word of God was changed into the nature of the flesh. For he (the Word) is unalterable and absolutely unchangeable and remains always the same as the scriptures say.[118]

Furthermore, in his "Letter to John of Antioch," Cyril declares that,

God the Word, who came down from above and from heaven, "emptied himself, taking the form of a slave", and was called son of man, though all the while he remained what he was, that is God (for he is unchangeable and immutable by nature), he is said to have come down from heaven, since he is now understood to be one with his own flesh.[119]

Pawl correctly argues that these citations indicate that Cyril did not understand divine immutability to be restricted to divine reliability, as the weak view claims. Disproving the weak view, however, is not the same thing as proving that Cyril had the strong view of immutability in mind.

When trying to understand how an author is using a term, context is vital. When the Council of Nicaea condemned those who affirmed "that the Son of God is subject to change or alteration," they were not anathematizing process theologians, or those seeking to refine the definition of immutability in modern contexts. Their condemnation was aimed at Arianism and the idea that the nature of the Word was not co-eternal or equally divine with the nature of the Father. Similarly, Cyril does not seem to be drawing from either the weak or the strong version of divine immutability. Rather, he specifies that there are ways in which the Word is said to "come down from above," empty himself, and take on a form, but that this does not entail his becoming something different from "God in nature and truth." The references the councils make to the unchanging divine nature are made in the context of defending the incarnation from accusations that it implies a change *of nature*—that the divine nature itself turns into something else. They need not be taken as references to a characteristic of immutability, defined as an absolute lack of change, within persons who possess or exist in the divine nature.

Cyril's letters are not only condemnations of Nestorius' arguments, they are also a defense of his own. Cyril condemned Nestorius for dividing the person of the Word based on the belief that two natures required two persons, but he also had to defend himself from Nestorius' charge that Cyril was guilty of confusing the natures and saying that the divine nature was passible.[120] With this accusation in mind, Cyril's argument that "we do not say that his flesh was turned into the nature of the godhead or that the unspeakable Word of God was changed into the nature of the flesh ... for he ... remains always the same as the scriptures say," can better be read as his defense against the charge of confusing the natures, than as an assertion of the Word's absolute lack of any type of change. Significantly, Cyril applies his argument to *both* the divine and the human natures. Not only was the godhead not changed into "the nature of the flesh," but the flesh was not "turned into the nature of the godhead," either. No one within the classical tradition has argued that a characteristic of strong immutability applies to flesh, but Cyril's denials of change applied to both the godhead and the flesh of the incarnation. Taking both assertions seriously leads to an "intermediate" view of immutability as the inability of one nature to be transformed into another.

An "intermediate" understanding of immutability as the inability of one nature to be transformed into another lies at the heart of conciliar Christology. The metaphysical understanding of salvation with which the councils were working was that Jesus saved by uniting the divine nature with the human nature that was in need of saving. If this union transformed human nature into something else rather than healing the nature itself, then the benefits of the union would not be transferable to other human beings. Similarly, if this union transformed divine nature into something else, then it would lose its power to save. The conciliar language about the lack of change of the divine nature occurs in contexts that assert that the incarnation did nothing to lessen the divinity of that nature. An intermediate view of immutability does not create logical incoherence because it applies to human nature as well, and therefore it does not rule out the kinds of change that are inherent in human life. At the same time, an intermediate view of immutability supports the theologically important idea that an unchanging divine faithfulness undergirds all of creation.

Finally, created *ousia* provides a way of understanding the attributes "incapable of death" and "capable of death" as logically coherent. Although individual instantiations of created *ousia* can be characterized by the same predicates that the coherence debates traditionally ascribe to human beings, created *ousia* as that which is shared by all of material reality transcends those predicates as well. For example, created *ousia* does not die, but continues to exist even as individual instantiations of created *ousia* pass away.[121] If immortal means incapable of death, then created *ousia* is immortal. Similarly, individual created beings are localized to a place, but created *ousia* itself encompasses all of creation—it is everywhere.[122] If omnipresence is given the positive definition of being present in every part of creation, then it would seem to apply to created *ousia*. Viewed in this way, the characteristics of created *ousia* are analogically related to, rather than logical contradictions of, the divine attributes that have been used to support logical challenges to the coherence of the incarnation.

Considering the ways that created *ousia* itself transcends the attributes that can properly characterize individual instantiations of created *ousia* provides a resolution to the coherence debates that does not require convoluted explorations of formal logic. A western scrub-jay, as an individual, is mortal, transient, and located in time and place. Partaking in created *ousia*, however, it can also be understood to transcend these characteristics and be incapable of death, everlasting, and omnipresent. There is no logical barrier to understanding that one entity can be simultaneously said to be both mortal and incapable of death, or bounded in space and omnipresent.

The way that debates over the coherence of the incarnation use language about both the divine and the human is inadequate for the topics that are being discussed. Divine transcendence means that some form of difference must be recognized when concepts are used across the divine/created divide, and the tradition has generally recognized that this is so—at least until it comes to discussing the logical (in)coherence of the incarnation. Similarly, a greater sensitivity to the complexity of material existence reveals that created *ousia* transcends those human attributes commonly invoked in challenges to the coherence of the incarnation. Created *ousia* does not create the same logical inconsistencies that a narrower focus on human nature does.

Although it may not resolve all of the issues involved in debates over the coherence of the incarnation, defining created *ousia* as "being involved in interdependent relationships of mutual transformation" and asserting that divinity is properly characterized by unchanging faithfulness provides an alternative to classical theism's portrayal of the logical conflict inherent in the doctrine of the incarnation. It demonstrates that creaturely attributes can be understood as both identical to those characteristics traditionally attributed to human beings and transcending those definitions as well. Thus, the claim that Jesus Christ was consubstantial with both the Father and with creation does not create a logical contradiction. This logical coherence, however, does not require a pantheistic claim that all of creation incarnates God. Christians can and do claim that the person of Jesus Christ uniquely possesses both divine and created *ousia*. Recovering the logic behind Nicaea's assertion that there are only two *ousiai* undermines attempts to use the doctrine of the incarnation to justify racial, gender-based, and ecological inequities. A further examination of the nature of created *ousia* responds to claims that it is incoherent to assert that Jesus Christ is both human and divine. In order to address the third category of christological problems, plausibility issues, the two-*ousiai* Christology proposed here still needs to address how the incarnation can affect all members of creation.

4

AND GOD BECAME A CREATURE

Considering created *ousia* as the shared condition of all of creation, characterized by plurality, interdependence, and mutual transformation, demonstrates that it is logically coherent for one person to partake of created *ousia* while also being divine. A two-*ousiai* Christology is not complete, however, without also addressing the question of what the incarnation accomplishes, or why the Word would assume such created *ousia* in the first place. This requires examining traditional understandings of the salvific effects of the incarnation as well as engaging Karl Barth's radically Christocentric understanding of election in order to discover how the incarnation can be universally effective.

Anselm's famous question, "Why did God become man?" (*Cur Deus Homo*) can be restated, "Why did God become a creature?" but the question remains. Conciliar Christologies have all presupposed that the purpose of the incarnation was "for us and for our salvation."[1] This led to the development of many "salvation Christologies" that describe the purpose of the incarnation as the salvation of humanity—or creation—from some deficiency. Some of these Christologies are infralapsarian, positing remediation of sin as the motivation for the incarnation, while others are supralapsarian and assume that the incarnation would have occurred whether or not human beings ever sinned.[2] Infralapsarian salvation Christologies have tended to repudiate the goodness of creation by treating the mutability or the interdependence of created *ousia* as the predicament from which we need saving, and supralapsarian ones improperly limit the significance of the incarnation to particularly human concerns regarding communion or perfection.[3] Both results undermine the traditional Christian claim that the incarnation has absolute and universal significance. Additionally, many salvation Christologies assume that the effects of the incarnation are only brought to those who hear, understand, and accept the story of Jesus—namely, Christians. This assumption leads to plausibility challenges that question the universal significance of an incarnation that excludes non-Christians from its benefits.[4] In contrast, a two-*ousiai* "creation Christology" affirms the absolute and universal significance of the incarnation, and it does so without providing support for the Christian chauvinism that has become increasingly unpalatable for a pluralistic and multi-religious world.[5]

THE PROBLEM(S) WITH SALVATION CHRISTOLOGIES

Apart from challenges to the logical coherence of the doctrine of creation, many still question the Christian claim that the Word becoming human in one particular person, at one particular place and time, could have absolute and universal significance. These challenges to the plausibility of the doctrine of the incarnation are rooted in genuine concerns about the limitations of special revelation. Such concerns arise not from the doctrine itself, but rather from preconceptions about how and why the incarnation functions in the lives of ordinary human beings. These preconceptions are shaped by anthropocentric assumptions that the incarnation occurred for human salvation, and that its efficacy is mediated through cognitive reception of revelation.[6]

Salvation has been described in many different ways, including salvation from death, corruptibility (or transformation), ignorance, punishment, bondage to sin, or estrangement (from God and/or one another). In accordance with the Christian tradition's habit of using multiple models and mixed metaphors to describe the work of the incarnation, these different descriptions are often invoked in tandem, indicating that they are not considered mutually exclusive descriptions of salvation.[7] One problem that most salvation Christologies share is that, regardless of the particular way in which salvation is described, the continuing condition of the world indicates that the incarnation did not achieve the results expected.[8] Whether salvation is understood as the defeat of death, the bringing of knowledge, freedom from sin, or reconciliation and restoration of full communion, human beings are still estranged, ignorant (at least of the true nature of the divine), sinful, and mortal. The birth, life, death, and resurrection of Jesus did not put an end to death or sin, despite the promises of Scripture. For Christians, the cognitive dissonance between the promises Scripture makes and the daily human experience leads to a number of different (although not mutually exclusive) methods for reconciling the two. One is to assert that these things have been accomplished through the incarnation already, but their consummation will only be experienced in the eschaton. By deferring the realization of salvation until after the end of the world, this renders scriptural promises non-falsifiable, but also ineffective, in this life. Another method of reconciliation, more popular in the eighteenth and nineteenth centuries, was to argue that the incarnation did bring these results, but that they take time to be made evident within creation. Scientific, cultural, religious, and political advancements were lifted up as evidence that the world was living into the reign of God. Such belief in the inevitable progress of society, however, became much more difficult to maintain during and after two world wars. A third approach privatizes these understandings of salvation. The individual might be freed from sin and reconciled to God, even if the world is not. The individual soul might gain immortality and a beatific vision of God, even if the rest of creation remained mortal and in ignorance. This approach allows the effects of the incarnation to be experienced in this life, although it obviously undermines claims for the incarnation's universal significance.

These problems can be addressed by positing another, non-soteriological reason for the incarnation. Doing so need not deny that it also accomplishes any of these salvific functions. Some may be affirmed as effects of the incarnation in individual lives without making them the foundation of the claim that it is absolutely and universally significant. It is possible that individuals are affected by the incarnation in different ways, that a number of people experiencing forgiveness, enlightenment, and reconciliation might spread these elements and shape the world in positive ways, and that there will be a new age in which old things are made new and perfect. Upholding the cosmic claim that the incarnation is immediately and universally effective, however, requires the work of the incarnation to be understood as something more than simply human salvation.

In addition to the dissonance between scriptural promises of salvation and lived experience, particular understandings of salvation may be criticized on other bases as well. The idea that creatures need to be saved from their mutability is based on the idea that humanity was created immortal and given a principle that made it impervious to corruption, ignoring the fact that death and decay were parts of the material world long before human beings evolved.[9] Considering that all of creation is subject to change, this understanding of salvation should be set aside on the basis of Christianity's affirmation of the goodness of creation. Participating in mutual transformation is characteristic of created *ousia*. The condition of being a good creature of God includes being subject to all kinds of transformation, and it is not something from which we need salvation. In addition to repudiating the goodness of created *ousia*, the idea that salvation means being rescued from mutability generates some absurd results when extended to the rest of creation.[10] It raises the question of whether cockroaches, dust mites, mosquitoes, lumps of coal, and Ebola viruses receive an immortal and immutable spiritual existence. If not, their exclusion from "salvation" undermines the Christian claim that the incarnation is universally significant, unless the incarnation accomplishes something else in addition to the granting of such an afterlife.

The understanding of salvation as the removal of ignorance is informed by and in turn reinforces theological and philosophical preoccupation with human rationality. Speaking theologically, the ignorance from which the incarnation is supposed to save us is not necessarily a lack of omniscience, but rather a lack of true knowledge about God.[11] A Christian commitment to the transcendence of God and the limitations of human language indicates that we cannot know God *in se*, at least not through natural means. Therefore, the knowledge Christians actually claim the incarnation brings is more limited. Rather than claiming to know God in God's self, many Christians claim that they have received the true knowledge necessary for salvation. All too often this leads Christians to act as though they alone have obtained this saving truth while non-Christians remain condemned.[12] Critics of the doctrine of the incarnation point out that it would be unjust for God to provide the message of salvation to some and not to others. Those who lived and died before Jesus could never have received a message that he uniquely brought.[13] Those who never hear the story of Jesus would not receive the message and those who are culturally conditioned to disbelieve such assertions about Jesus would be less likely to accept them. They would therefore be lost simply because of where they were born and raised. Unfortunately, this understanding of salvation has been used to support slavery in the past and cultural colonialism into the present.[14] Many Christians view it as their duty to create the cultural conditions for learning about Jesus throughout the world, and they believe the importance of doing so outweighs the harms caused by such colonialism. In addition to condemning the harms of colonialism, critics of the plausibility of the incarnation raise another objection: if there is intelligent life on other planets, it has also not received this salvific revelation and would therefore be condemned as well.[15] Even without considering the possibility of extraterrestrial life, not all of creation functions cognitively in such a way that "possessing knowledge" is an apt description of what it does. Furthermore, there are certainly people born into and raised in Christian families and communities that lack the cognitive capacity to understand assertions about Jesus, and who are therefore unable to either accept or reject them in any meaningful way. If Christians are to affirm the absolute and universal significance of the incarnation, that meaning cannot be lodged with the cognitive appropriation of certain assertions about Jesus.

Understanding salvation as forgiveness for sin avoids these particular problems. If the problem from which creation needs saving is divine judgment for sin, then the incarnation might achieve forgiveness of sin without the recipients' cognitive appropriation of that fact. Unfortunately, even these understandings of salvation undermine the claim that the incarnation is absolutely and universally significant. Because Christians have largely affirmed that only humans and other rational beings (like angels) are capable of sin, salvation as rescue from punishment for or bondage to sin limits the significance of the incarnation to such rational beings. Christians have rarely asserted that rocks, trees, ants, and birds sin.[16] The epistle to the Romans provides a biblical argument that although the rest of creation may not commit sin, it nevertheless suffers under the sinfulness of human beings and thus needs rescue from the effects of sin, if not forgiveness for its own sin.[17] This argument, however, places human beings and human salvation as mediators of the effects of both sin and salvation to the rest of creation, depriving the incarnation of its immediate universal effectiveness. It thus undermines the absolute and universal significance of the incarnation, making its effects dependent on the response and remediation of others while also relegating those effects to some unknown future.

The final way of understanding salvation as overcoming estrangement is more promising, although still problematically anthropocentric. Historically, this view of salvation has taken both infralapsarian and supralapsarian forms. In the infralapsarian form, the incarnation overcomes humanity's estrangement from God that occurs as a result of human sin. In the incarnation, Jesus mediates reconciliation between God and humanity. Again, both the problem of estrangement through sin and the solution of reconciliation would be limited to human beings alone. In the supralapsarian form, the incarnation is required to achieve the communion that God originally intended with creation and it would have been necessary even if human beings had not sinned.[18] This perspective is the most promising of those offered by salvation Christologies and can be reconciled with a two-*ousiai* Christology. Although it is not clear that biological limestone or Big Bluestem fall short of the glorious communion that God intends for them, there is no obstacle to assuming that they might exist in better communion with God and the rest of creation. Because of the interdependence of created *ousia*, if any creature is estranged from God, the warp and weft of all creation might be strained out of perfect communion.[19] Salvation as overcoming estrangement or achieving divine communion addresses concerns about the anthropocentric focus of most salvation Christologies, but the first problem still remains. It is evident that the incarnation has not actually overcome such estrangement. The world does not yet exist in perfect harmony with itself or perfect communion with God.

Thus Christians are left with three options. They can assume that the incarnation accomplishes salvation now for a limited number of creatures or in a limited way, they can assume that the incarnation opens a path for universal salvation but that it will not be consummated in this life, or they can base their claims of Christ's universal significance on something other than salvation. These options need not be mutually exclusive. The claim that the incarnation has accomplished something of universal significance beyond what has been traditionally envisioned as salvation need not exclude, for instance, the claims that it also accomplishes present salvation for some and opens a path for universal reconciliation in the future. Rather, this third option bases the universal significance of the incarnation on something already accomplished and effective for the whole cosmos, while leaving open room for understanding the specific effects of the incarnation on particular creatures in different ways appropriate to their individual circumstances—which may well include human salvation in some or all of the ways it has been traditionally understood.[20]

CREATION CHRISTOLOGY

Although salvation Christologies have dominated Christian theological reflection, creation Christologies upholding Christ's universal significance for the entire cosmos trace their roots to biblical sources. Colossians 1:15-20 names Jesus Christ "the firstborn of all creation" and claims that "in him all things in heaven and on earth were created . . . all things have been created through him and for him. He himself is before all things, and in him all things hold together. . . . in him all the fullness of God was pleased to dwell, and through him God was pleased to reconcile to himself all things." The prologue to John asserts that "all things came into being through him, and without him not one thing came into being" (1:3). These and other passages indicate that at least part of the work of the Word of God involves creation itself. This led many early theologians to advance an understanding of the Cosmic Christ that encompasses more than purely human concerns.[21] Although it fell out of popular discourse with the Protestant Reformations' emphasis on the *pro nobis* of the incarnation and the increasingly individualistic understandings of salvation that developed in their wake, the idea of the Cosmic (or Universal) Christ was revived in response to the existential threats posed to humanity from nuclear armament and environmental degradation in the twentieth and twenty-first centuries.[22] It was in the post-Hiroshima threat of more nuclear war that Joseph Sittler drew on Colossians 1:15-20 in order to propose Christian unity in light of cosmic Christology.[23] Drawing on Irenaeus' concept of the recapitulation *mundi* and Sittler's writings, Moltmann similarly argues that the work of Christ can only be properly conceived as cosmic in scope.[24] More recently, this has been taken up in discussions of deep incarnation—the idea that the incarnation is not limited to human nature alone, but extends into the depth of evolutionary history as well.[25]

Deep incarnation draws on those biblical texts that affirm the universal significance of the incarnation to argue that the Word does not just assume a particular human being, but enters into the matrix of all of creation.[26] Elizabeth Johnson has expanded this notion to include "deep crucifixion" and "deep resurrection" as well.[27] In the face of creaturely suffering that results from causes other than human sin, deep incarnation and deep resurrection have implications for theodicies, portraying the incarnation as a form of divine accompaniment and solidarity with God's suffering creatures.[28] Because proponents of deep incarnation recognize that suffering is not usually the result of human sin, but rather the natural consequence of developed nervous systems and evolutionary pressure (and is therefore part of the created condition), they cast the incarnation as God's response to this supralapsarian suffering, a response that can redeem and transform that suffering in the future.[29] Although deep incarnation pushes against anthropocentrism by including evolutionary suffering in theological reflection, its salvation-oriented emphasis on creaturely suffering tends to limit the effects of the incarnation to creatures that experience pain, still undermining its universal significance (i.e., it is not clear that deep incarnation connects the work of Christ to biological limestone, or other non-sentient members of creation). Nevertheless, by challenging the "dermal metaphysics" that neglects the interdependence of all of creation, deep incarnation resonates with a two-*ousiai* creation Christology.[30] Similarly, a two-*ousiai* creation Christology can provide the metaphysical framework missing from claims that the incarnation delves beyond human nature to something that unites all of creation.[31]

Karl Barth's doctrine of election provides the strongest modern articulation of a creation Christology, although his proposal remains decidedly anthropocentric.[32] Despite this anthropocentrism, the logic of Barth's understanding of election and its relationship to creation, when corrected by certain claims from deep incarnation, provides a strong foundation for a two-*ousiai* creation Christology. Drawing together doctrines of creation, Christology, and election, Barth's argument, painfully condensed, is that God's decision to be for another (i.e., God's election of what is other than God) entails the primordial decision to become incarnate while also providing the grounds for creation. Barth follows a dominant strand of Christian tradition in assuming that although God had no need of creation (because God's intratrinitarian being is a self-sufficient community of love), God created the cosmos anyway.[33] God creates "in order not to be alone and to have this other quite different reality before, with Him, and near Him."[34] For Barth, this creation is grounded in divine election, in God's decision to be with and for God's creature(s). Although nothing forces God to make this election, God chooses to constrain Godself and become a companion to God's creature(s).[35] This does not mean, however, that God encounters another and then decides to become a companion to it. According to Barth, Christian theology does not have to do with a divine being who first decides to create a world and then decides to enter into a relationship with it.[36] Instead, God's election is the "meaning and content" of creation.[37] Creation exists only as a consequence of divine election.[38]

This election is not, for Barth, primarily an election of creation, or even of humanity as such. Rather it is the election of one particular man, Jesus of Nazareth. The whole history of God and the created world has "no independent signification. It takes place in the interests of the primal history which is played out between God *and this one man* and his people."[39] Jesus is the one that God elects, and it is only through him and in him that others are also elected.[40] He is himself the election, the relation, the covenant between God and humanity.[41] Everything else, including all of creation, flows from and serves God's purposes in the election of Jesus.[42] In circling back from creation to election to the incarnation, Barth collapses linear understandings of salvation history. Rather than God creating, then becoming incarnate in response to some defect within creation, and finally through that incarnation electing certain people for salvation, God elects Jesus in the incarnation, then through Jesus God elects the rest of creation, which ultimately explains why God created in the first place.[43] According to Barth's logic, the work of the incarnation is primarily that of being the covenant-partner elected by God and electing God in return. Only through God's election of Jesus do creation generally and humanity particularly come into being.[44] This means that creatures are elected by God before they exist, that they are created in order for God to be a companion and covenant-partner to them. It makes the incarnation, or at least God's decision to become incarnate, the foundation of created existence.[45]

Barth's description of election as the divine will to be for another relates to supralapsarian salvation Christologies that envision the work of the incarnation as creating the possibility for divine communion with humanity. After all, "willing to be for another" is an apt description of the love that lies at the heart of such communion. Barth's proposal is distinctive, however, in that it places this love for creatures prior to, and as the cause for, creation. According to this logic, "willing to be for another" when no other exists, "willing to be for another" in such a way that the other is called into being, is the divine prerogative. Creatures can be for others that already exist, but only the divine can actually constitute another through this willing. Divine love as the "willing to be for another" is the foundation of the doctrine of creation *ex nihilo*.[46] But if Christianity is going to continue to affirm the absolutely gracious nature of material creation, then this divine will to be for another must be satisfied without recourse to the world as a necessary object of divine love. This can be done by following Barth's assertion that divine election applies primarily to the incarnation, and to creation only derivatively, through the incarnate One.

Other supralapsarian Christologies create a theological problem by making something so fundamental to the Christian understanding of God—that God is the one who becomes incarnate within creation—merely functional within the history of God's dealings with humanity. Most supralapsarian Christologies are rooted in the idea that although creation was made good, it was not made perfect.[47] Even before human beings sinned, they lacked something necessary for the fulfillment of their ultimate destiny. The incarnation would always have been necessary for the consummation of creation. Therefore, the incarnation is a tool for the fulfillment of human destiny. If God is who God is in order to bring humanity to perfection, then anthropocentrism has finally dislodged theocentrism. Whereas most supralapsarian Christologies treat the embodied expression of God as a response to a need within created reality, Barth's proposal clearly treats creation as the derivative effect of divine incarnation. It leaves no room for subordinating the incarnation to God's plans for humanity, but rather makes humanity itself a function of God's decision to become incarnate. That decision logically precedes the foundation of the world, and creation occurs only through it.

This does not mean that Barth's proposal is without challenges of its own. Treating the incarnation as the basis for creation creates a conceptual difficulty because effects are not generally thought to precede their causes.[48] Jesus was born at a particular point in time, but creation and a great deal of human history existed prior to that time. This raises the question of how the Word's becoming incarnate in the person of Jesus could provide the foundation for the existence of, say, Jesus' mother and grandmother, who obviously existed prior to the conception of Jesus.[49] One solution to this problem involves an understanding of God as timeless. Proponents of divine timelessness (or atemporalism) hold that God's eternity does not mean that God lives forever, but that God's life does not have a past and a future as the lives of human beings do.[50] Instead, God lives in a timeless present. According to this argument, one can say that the Word is "timelessly God Incarnate."[51] Alternatively, one could assert with Barth that as the Lord of Time, Jesus' time is always present, or that in the resurrection and ascension the life (and work) of Jesus is made contemporaneous with all of created time.[52] Another proposed solution involves a part-whole argument. If the Word is understood as one part of the whole in the incarnation, and the body and soul of Jesus as other parts of that whole, the Word could always be understood as incarnate because what would happen at the conception of Jesus had already been determined by God.[53] There are many ways for Christians to affirm that what occurs in the incarnation can be effective throughout created time—including before the birth of Jesus, and even before the evolution of humanity.

Although Barth's anthropocentrism leads him to view creation's participation in election and covenant as derivative and occurring only through humanity's participation therein, created *ousia* provides a way to understand the incarnation as universally effective without privileging humanity as mediators of its effects. As Barth argues, God chooses not to be alone, but constrains Godself in order to be a companion to another. The incarnation is the event in which the Word becomes another for God, and in which the other for whom God can "be for" comes into existence. This otherness cannot consist in a simple replication of the divine *ousia*. Instead, it calls forth created *ousia*, that which is not God, from nothing. In doing so, both the substance and the relationality of creation—relationship *to* God and *between* its individual members—are established. Divine love as it is manifest in the calling forth of created *ousia*, hypostasized in the incarnation, means that ontological multiplicity exists, that God is not God alone, but is with and for God's creature. This provides a theological affirmation of the preliminary definition of created *ousia* developed earlier. Created *ousia* consists of an interdependent plurality of beings. If the foundation of created *ousia* is God's election to be for another, then that foundation is multiplicity—*being another*—and interdependence—being *for* another. With such a foundation, created *ousia* does not exist as a solitary entity, but reverberates in the creation of light and dark, sea and land, and the billions of creatures teeming in the water, over the land, and in the air.

THE METAPHYSICS OF A TWO-*OUSIAI* CHRISTOLOGY

Understanding how the incarnation can be universally effective requires some further examination of metaphysical assumptions. As the field focused on "being" as such, metaphysics addresses questions of what is most fundamental to being, or what is the most real reality, whether that is some universal form, the individuals with whom we interact, or the relationships that exist between entities.[54] The early church seemed to be operating under a substance metaphysics, or what Paul Janz refers to as "metaphysical realism," in which substance is fundamental. It is not clear whether early theologians understood the most fundamental substance to be the universals in which multiple individuals participate or the individuals about whom generalizations can be made.[55] The problem is that such debates about whether individuals or universals are more primal seem to overlook the irreducible interdependence of the two. The generalizable, or universal, does not exist without two or more particulars, but neither do two or more particulars exist without something generalizable between them. Both individuals and universals are real, and neither need assume a conceptual priority over the other. Furthermore, neither concept would be strictly applicable to a single entity, entirely alone. It would not be a particular instantiation of any generality, nor would there be any generality to be made about that single entity. Once there is multiplicity, however, there will be some things that the multiple entities share—the general, and some things that they do not, which differentiates them as individuals. Neither needs to be considered more or less real than the other. As the shared condition of all creatures, the mutually transforming interdependence that characterizes created *ousia* can be considered both a universal in which all individual creatures participate and the individual instantiations of that trait found in every creature. It is both present wherever (and whenever) creatures exist, and transcending individual creatures as they are transformed from one particular body into another.

Having been developed largely on the basis of early christological claims, which were steeped in substantive ontologies, the two-*ousiai* Christology proposed is certainly coherent with substance metaphysics. Instead of alleging that the Word brings divine nature into hypostatic union with particularly human nature (in the individual incarnation of Jesus Christ), this proposal suggests that the Word brings divine *ousia* into hypostatic union with created *ousia* in the individual incarnation of Jesus Christ. *Ousia*, however, need not be understood solely as a universal shared substance in the same way that the council of Chalcedon understood human nature. In addition to age-old debates about the relationship of the individual to the universal, there has been a modern turn from substance to relational ontology.[56] Rather than questioning whether individuals or universals are more fundamental, this debate turns to whether relationships or individuals are more fundamental to being. Like debates over the primacy of individuals or universals in substance metaphysics, this conflict seems to overlook the irreducible interdependence of both relationship and substance. There can be no relationships without beings, and there cannot be more than one being without relationship. There is no such thing as one solitary entity, existing entirely alone, and this means that there is relationship of some sort.[57] Again, neither relationship nor substance need be thought of as more fundamentally real than the other—each implies the other.[58]

Because the preliminary definition of created *ousia* itself invokes relationship to define what is shared by all of creation (i.e., mutually transformative interdependence), it demonstrates how substance and relationship can both be considered fundamental. If multiplicity necessarily follows from the divine decision to be for another, and to have another for whom God could be, then relationality is foundational for substantial existence. Similarly, if a substance distinct from God necessarily follows from the divine decision to be for another, then substance is foundational for genuine relationship. Neither substance nor relationship exists without the other. According to this understanding, everything that is created, everything other than God, derives its being from God's will to be for another. Nothing has existence on any other basis. God's will to be for another is enacted in the incarnation, which grounds all other extra-divine relationships. The incarnation is the expression of that divine will: the Word becomes another for the Father by partaking in created *ousia*. But the incarnation is not just the assumption of another substance, as though created *ousia* had some existence before the Word assumed it. Created *ousia* is called into being from nothing in the Word's assumption of it. The incarnation thus creates created *ousia*. As the created manifestation of divine love, this *ousia* is also "for another." It does not exist in isolation, but is fruitful and multiplies in countless different trajectories as it becomes the myriad of particular created bodies that all share in this being for others.

A PLAUSIBLE RESOLUTION

This two-*ousiai* creation Christology asserts that the being—the very existence—of creation itself *is* the universal significance of the incarnation. Because the incarnation calls created *ousia* into existence in the first place and provides it with the stability necessary to persist in ongoing relationships of mutual transformation, it affects every part of creation without limit and without mediation. This answers plausibility challenges to the incarnation that hold it is unbelievable that one particular person living in one particular time and place could have the universal significance that Christians have traditionally claimed for Jesus Christ. Such challenges are based on the limitations of special revelation: that the life of Jesus reveals certain knowledge necessary for salvation and the incarnation can thus only be effective for those who have heard and accepted the story of that life. If the primary work of the incarnation is pedagogical, either to teach creatures how to be better or to teach them how to know God, then these limitations do undermine human concepts of justice.[59] If God condemns those creatures that do not believe certain things or follow certain rules for either their beliefs or behavior, but only reveals the things to be believed or the rules to be obeyed to some, then God is not acting in ways we understand as fair and the incarnation is not universally effective.

A two-*ousiai* creation Christology, however, does not turn on either revelation or cognitive appropriation of that revelation. Instead, the incarnation grants both existence and God's companionship to all of creation, including all that existed "prior" to the birth of Jesus as well as all that exists "after" his ascension. These gifts were given to those disciples that traveled and talked and ate with him, and they were given to the atoms that existed in the reaches of space farthest from him. If the incarnation gives creation both existence and God's friendship, then it is not given to an already existing world, as though it were an intervention to fix some imperfection within creation. It is the foundation of existence as such. It is the gift given to that which does not exist, a gift that constitutes its very existence. Every moment that anything "is," it is only as this gift.

Those conditions that characterize twenty-first-century understandings of the cosmos therefore stand as no barrier to the plausibility of the incarnation's universal significance. The fact that the universe is much bigger than early Christians believed it was has no impact on whether the Word's assumption of created *ousia* could be significant for every atom within it. Because the incarnation's universal effectiveness is based on the Word's assumption of created *ousia*, rather than on revelation, the possibility that sentient life which has never heard the story of Jesus might exist in some other galaxy does not impinge on the incarnation's significance. Because this effect of the incarnation is not mediated through cognitive appropriation of certain theological propositions, it does not support Christian chauvinism that disparages other religions, nor does it deny the possibility that such other religions might also contain divine revelation. A two-*ousiai* creation Christology provides no support for viewing those incapable of cognitive appropriation of theological propositions as somehow further from the effects of the incarnation or less beloved by God than are rational human beings. It thus provides a way to understand the incarnation as absolutely, universally, uniquely, and immediately significant without providing grounds for the justice, coherence, and plausibility challenges that have been raised against the doctrine in the past.

5
CREATED TOGETHER

"In the beginning was the Word, and the Word was with God, and the Word was God.... All things came into being through him, and without him not one thing came into being" (John 1:1, 3). The first three verses of John contain the mystery of two-*ousiai* Christology. Difference and identity lie at the heart of the Christian faith, for the Word both *was* God and was *with* God. The Word became flesh and dwelt among us in order to become an object for God's love. As Cyril asserted, the Word "remained what he was, God in nature and truth," and yet he also became incarnate as a creature in order to be with God, calling all created being into existence in the process.[1] The incarnation of the Word in the person of Jesus is absolutely, unrepeatably, universally significant, because it provides the foundation for the existence of everything that is.

The two-*ousiai* Christology developed here answers the objections that the doctrine of the incarnation supports Christian injustices and that it is incoherent and implausible. The tasks of retrieval, deconstruction, and reconstruction remain incomplete, however. Reconstructing a two-*ousiai* Christology raises new objections, questions, and avenues for further theological exploration. Some Christians may object by claiming that viewing every part of creation as an absolutely beloved creature of God reduces human dignity in unacceptable ways. Some may argue that the fact that the Word became incarnate as a human being proves that human beings are of greater worth than other creatures. Others may wonder whether a two-*ousiai* Christology leaves any room for Christians to talk about salvation at all. Still others, inclined towards accepting a two-*ousiai* Christology, may be curious about its ethical and theological implications.

One contribution that systematic theology makes to wider theological reflection is the core conviction that all theological claims are inherently intertwined and the revision of one claim necessarily entails rethinking the others. Thus, no theological argument can ever have the final word. Each instead offers a new starting point for Christians to begin thinking through their beliefs again. In order to set the stage for this future endeavor of reconsidering other claims from a two-*ousiai* perspective, three tasks remain: addressing persistent anthropocentric objections to the elevation of creaturely dignity, sketching some preliminary thoughts on the theological implications of the arguments advanced here, and examining the capacities that need to be developed if Christians are to expand their moral considerations to include all of creation in the ways a two-*ousiai* Christology implies they should.

HUMAN DIGNITY

Although this proposal proceeded by bracketing out particularly human concerns in order to explore a more inclusive Christology, this bracketing process does not eliminate human concerns, nor does it render them irrelevant to theology. Rather, removing those brackets and reintroducing concerns about human dignity lead to two potential objections to the proposed two-*ousiai* Christology. The first is that, by elevating other creatures, it diminishes human beings. The second is that the fact that the Word did become incarnate as a human being proves that human beings are of greater worth than other creatures.

Infinite Love

Some might object that if God does not love human beings more than God loves other creatures, the grounds of human dignity are undermined, if not eliminated. This argument seems to be rooted in the assumption that love is a finite quantity that must be divvied up among the objects of that love. If God loves other creatures more than Christians have traditionally assumed, then God must love human beings less than they have assumed. The problem with this argument is that it places a finite limit on divine love, assuming that God does not have the capacity to love and cherish every single creature that does, has, or ever will exist to the same degree that God has traditionally been assumed to love and cherish human beings—or at least the elect among us. This stems from an anthropomorphism that projects human characteristics onto the divine. Although Christians understand that God has the capacity to care for all of humanity, from the worst sinner to the greatest saint, without allocating divine love on the basis of individual merit, many still seem to doubt that God could have the same capacity to love all of creation in the same way.

This problem likely arises because we have no creaturely analog for divine love. Many human beings experience compassion fatigue. We can love one another, but we can also "burn out" and become incapacitated when we care too much about too many people in a world of such immense suffering. Professionals who deal with traumatic situations on a daily basis learn to distance themselves from those they are helping, to create boundaries in order to avoid secondary trauma to themselves. The idea of loving not only our own families, or nations, or races, or even species, but also every member of every species and every inanimate body as well, loving them with the same concern that a parent loves their child, is overwhelming to the human imagination. Therefore, many assume that the divine is similarly incapable of this feat. This assumption improperly applies a creaturely characteristic univocally to the divine. Within our world of finitude, all resources have their limits, including our own energy and affection. As a result we tend to value things according to their importance to us in this world of scarcity. Applied univocally to the divine-world relation, this implies that if the dormouse and the mosquito are God's beloved children, God's love for humanity will be diluted.

Of course, any parent who claims to love their children equally but in different ways appropriate to their own unique personalities, needs, and abilities understands that love need not be a zero-sum game. God can love human beings enough to be willing to become incarnate, suffer, and die in order that we might be, and God can also love the mosquito enough to be willing to become incarnate, suffer, and die in order that it might be. Hierarchies of value are only necessary if one envisions an interventionist God that slays the lion in order to defend the hunter, a God that prefers certain individuals or species to others and acts in light of those preferences. Setting aside the assumption that God intends human flourishing *at the expense of* other creatures, there is no need to imagine that human beings are more important, more valued, or more beloved than any other creature. Avoiding this assumption, however, does not require the depreciation of human life. God can love the prodigal son without loving the elder brother any less.

Expanding our concepts of divine love to encompass all of creation follows Christianity's egalitarian impulses. It recognizes that human dignity is rooted *not* in the specific capacities or deeds of a particular human being, or the capacities or deeds of the species as a whole, but rather in the gracious love that God bestows on God's creatures. Against distorted justifications of colonial oppression, white supremacy, and patriarchy, this strand of the tradition reminds Christians that, in the words of Paul, "while we were yet sinners, Christ died for us" (Rom 5:8). It denies the lie that superior wealth, strength, or power indicates a greater value to the divine. It asserts that one group does not need to bolster its self-esteem by claiming superiority to another, but that each can find its worth in the unfailing love of God. It bases human dignity on God's care for individual human beings, a divine care that does not wax and wane based on how well an individual manifests some privileged characteristic. This divine love also affirms each individual's unique relationship to God. Each relationship is unique because it is a relationship between God and the individual being in all of its particularity. Every human being has a unique relationship to the divine, but so does every non-human being as well. God's love extends universally to every creature, but God's relationship to each is unique.

The "Proof" of the Incarnation

Even if human dignity remains the same, rooted in God's love for each human being, some might still object that the incarnation itself proves that human beings are more important than other creatures. The problem with this objection is that it is circular: it begins with the assumption that human beings are more important, and then uses the incarnation as a human being as evidence to support that assumption. This circularity can be seen with similar arguments that it was only fitting for the Word to have become incarnate as a man, rather than a woman. Those arguments began with the assumption that men possessed greater dignity than women, and then used Jesus' status as a man to justify their earlier assumptions. As in that case, there is no way to prove or disprove the argument entirely. Advancing a number of alternative explanations, however, undermines the anthropocentric or androcentric assumption with which the argument began. There are many other possible explanations for why the Word might have chosen to become incarnate as a human being, explanations that do not support anthropocentric biases. An examination of these explanations should demonstrate that there is no reason to grant deference to the chauvinistic interpretations of the humanity of Jesus that have been traditionally influential.

Divine Condescension

The first alternative explanation cuts to the quick of anthropocentric assumptions. Following the kenotic logic of Philippians 2:6-8, this explanation assumes that the Word became incarnate as a human being because humans are the lowliest creatures, rather than the loftiest.[2] Without venturing into debates about the implications this passage might have for divine attributes, most interpreters agree that it describes the incarnation as the ultimate divine condescension.[3] According to this passage, in the incarnation the Word gave up its honored status of "equality with God" and took on instead the lowly status of emptiness and slavery—humanity. Not content with that level of humility, the passage goes on to note that even as a human Jesus was humbled further by the shame of his death by crucifixion. The logic of this passage leaves no room for judging the form of the incarnation—the form of human likeness—as something of great value or importance. Rather, it seems to imply that humanity possesses the lowliest stature the Word could have assumed. The depth of divine condescension, is demonstrated not just by becoming material, but by becoming particularly *human*.

This logic reverses the anthropocentric assumption that Jesus' humanity indicates the innate superiority of human beings to other members of creation. Instead, it would seem that Jesus' humanity indicates our inferiority—in deciding to "be for another" by becoming incarnate the Word also becomes incarnate as the lowliest of material bodies. Although the Christian tradition has emphasized the Word's condescension in becoming human, usually it has held back from equating humanity with the nadir of emptiness and slavery. Many have argued that it was only fitting for the Word to become incarnate as a human being because of our inherent dignity.[4] Such arguments recognize a qualitative divide between the divine and humanity while insisting on a similar, qualitative rather than quantitative, divide between humanity and other creatures. These arguments strain logic, insisting as they do that the Word displayed the power of divinity in weakness, the wisdom of divinity in foolishness, the greatness of divinity in condescension, by becoming the best, wisest, and greatest material creature possible. The logic of divine self-emptying instead implies that in the incarnation, the divine descended to the depths of creation, that in becoming a man the Word emptied itself of divine dignity.

There are a number of things of which one might accuse humanity to justify its status as the lowest, rather than the highest, of creatures. We have rejected our interdependence, rebelled against our Creator, imagined ourselves capable of re-creating a better creation than the one we were given. We take pleasure in cruelty towards each other and towards other creatures. We violate the integrity of others—both other humans and other creatures—by habitually forcing them to do our bidding. The list could go on. These are not the sins of every society, nor are they the sins of every individual within a given society, but they do reflect common human impulses towards anthropocentrism and egocentrism that exceed those we find in other species.

This alternative provides a helpful counter-balance to the centuries of arguments that human beings must be greater than all other creatures because the Word became incarnate as a human being. It demonstrates that without the anthropocentric presumption that human beings are the greatest creatures to begin with, there is no reason to conclude that the Word's becoming incarnate as a human indicates such greatness. However, resisting anthropocentric biases does not require that one become a self-hating human, viewing ourselves as the worst of the worst, the nadir of creaturely existence. This explanation retains a hierarchy of valuation among creatures that is problematic if one begins with the assumption that all of creation—including human beings—is beloved by God. Rather than simply reversing the hierarchy and placing humanity in the lowest place, the second alternative explanation focuses on the fittingness of the incarnation according to need rather than according to dignity.

Concession to Need

This second explanation of why the Word became incarnate as a human being does not rely on a hierarchy of created value, appealing instead to human need. It has traditionally been tied to infralapsarian Christologies that assume that the purpose of the incarnation is to address human sin.[5] According to this logic, human beings could only be freed from our captivity to sin, or only justified from our guilt, through the agency of one who was also a human being. This is not incompatible with a two-*ousiai* Christology that portrays the purpose of the incarnation as becoming another for God—the particular form in which the Word became incarnate could still be governed by the greater needs of one species. This offers a way to understand the humanity of the incarnation as a concession to human need even if the effects of the incarnation stretch beyond humanity to every member of creation.

According to the proposed two-*ousiai* Christology, the primary effect of the incarnation is that it provides the foundation for created being, establishing the "other" for whom God can be. However, the effects of the incarnation need not be limited to this first work alone. It continues to provide the stability and the creativity that sustains creation throughout its many transformations. The incarnation provides the matrix for existence as we know it, the pattern by which material bodies interact. Most creatures live and move and have their being within this matrix, blending within the pattern of creation. Having not rebelled against their places in the cosmos, they have no need to repent and they need no remedial lessons in how they should behave. Many human beings, however, have denied their place within creation and tried to set themselves apart from the patterns of transformation that characterize created *ousia*. We have frequently been unwilling or unable to perceive the limits that should constrain our behavior, limits written into our created being itself. Therefore, we need to be corrected, to be given a model tailored to our limited perspectives.

Under this reasoning one might say that the incarnation could provide the pattern of created reality by taking on any creaturely form, but that human beings would refuse to conform to the pattern of interdependence unless it was presented in the form of a human being.[6] Objectively, this would not change our being—our existence would still be grounded in the divine decision to be for creation, and it would still be shaped by the interdependent nature of that creation. Subjectively, however, human beings might not perceive, accept, or receive the gifts that the incarnation provides, but rather continue in our rebellion against interdependence, remaining painfully at odds with the nature of material existence, unless the lesson was presented in terms we could understand.[7] This alternative explains why it might be fitting for the Word to become incarnate without either appealing to the greater dignity of human beings or positing humanity as the lowliest of creatures.

Arbitrary

Finally, it is possible that the Word's decision to become incarnate as a human being is entirely arbitrary. The work of the incarnation could have been accomplished through a hypostatic union with any creature, a possibility that Tertullian raises (without endorsing) in his arguments against Marcion: "Suppose that in point of fact he had wanted to be born of a wolf or a ewe or a cow and put on the body of some animal, wild or domestic, to proclaim the kingdom of heaven?"[8] Possessing all of the characteristics that make a body a member of one particular species or another is necessary in order for the Word to become incarnate, participating in the matrix of the material world. However, *which* particular characteristics are taken on could be irrelevant to the intention(s) of the Word in becoming incarnate. Once again, this explanation extends the logic of feminist critiques of the patriarchal essentialization of Jesus' maleness. As Johnson argues, sex is a constitutive part of Jesus' identity without reflecting anything about the relative value or need of males in comparison to females.[9] Jesus could not be a generic human, devoid of hypostatic properties, and so he had eye color and sex and hair color. None of these, however, necessarily reflect anything of soteriological significance. Similarly, Jesus could not be a generic creature, of no type and with no characteristics, and so he can be a human without that humanity necessarily reflecting anything of soteriological significance. There is a need for the Word to partake in created *ousia* for anything to exist, but the particular form of created *ousia* that the Word becomes need not tell us anything more about that form.

This (non)explanation undermines anthropocentrism by denying that the particular form of the incarnation indicates anything about God's valuing of similar forms of creatures. After all, the tradition has not ascribed a higher worth to humans who possess the same height, eye color, or mathematical abilities as Jesus did. This is likely because such characteristics are seen as different capacities within what was assumed to be the soteriologically significant category of humanity. If the matter is reframed so that no species distinctions are viewed as soteriologically significant, then the species that the Word assumed would become as irrelevant to the efficacy of the incarnation as these other characteristics have long been viewed.

It is unnecessary for human beings to find *the* definitive reason that the incarnation occurred in human form. Although each of these alternative explanations appeal to the underlying goal of resisting anthropocentric assumptions, they are not an exhaustive exploration of the possible reasons the Word became incarnate as a human being. What they do is demonstrate that when anthropocentric assumptions that the incarnation demonstrates God's greater esteem for human beings over against other creatures are not given a presumption of correctness, the incarnation itself does not automatically serve as evidence for such a divine preference.

THEOLOGICAL IMPLICATIONS

In addition to issues involving theological anthropology, a two-*ousiai* Christology raises questions about sin, salvation, and the doctrine of the Trinity. Because this Christology began with the assumption that the incarnation affects the entire created universe, rather than the assumption that it occurred only "for us and for our salvation," it has not engaged questions of human sinfulness and salvation in the same ways that other christological developments have. This need not, however, imply that there is no such thing as sin, nor that the incarnation is uninvolved in human salvation. Instead, it requires re-thinking how Christians describe the human predicament if mutability, mortality, and interdependence are good features of created being, rather than evils from which we need saving.

Sin

The Christian doctrine of creation definitively claims that human beings are not self-made. They are rather, as Schleiermacher observed, absolutely dependent upon the "whence" from which they have come.[10] Although Schleiermacher claims that this feeling of *absolute* dependence only relates to the transcendent divine, human beings are also dependent on the other beings that make up creation. We are dependent upon the creatures we consume through both respiration and digestion, and we are derivatively dependent on the creatures upon whom those creatures depend. Without food, water, or oxygen, we would quickly sicken and die. This dependence upon not only a divine Creator, but also on the "lowly" creatures we consume can be hard to acknowledge in societies that value the relative independence of the affluent. Christians have long assumed that that the "corruptibility" we experience in this dependence was not part of God's intention for humanity, but rather was the result of sin.[11] Salvation would therefore restore humanity to its privileged position of incorruptibility, removing it from the transforming influence of other material bodies. This idea developed into common understandings of salvation as an escape from the conditions of created being, to a condition in which human beings will be eternally fixed, no longer capable of being moved or influenced by any other creatures, and exempt from further creaturely transformation. This escapism views characteristics that are inherent in created *ousia*—mutability and interdependence—as evils from which we need to be saved. However, a perspective that assumes the goodness of created *ousia* views the human predicament differently.

Assuming the goodness of created *ousia* does not mean ignoring the presence of evil within the created order. Rather, it means viewing such evil not as the result of interdependence as such, but instead as an imbalance between the integrity of individual bodies and their dependence on one another. The tension between "being" (or "being for oneself") and "being for another" creates a web of interrelations. This web is distorted by those who refuse to acknowledge their dependence on others while simultaneously violating the integrity of those others. Such sinful creatures take from the matrix of creation more than they return to it, dissipating the energy of other material bodies in activities that do nothing to increase the capacities and resilience of the whole. This imbalance can be seen in purely human relationships as people with power direct resources to their own luxuries while people with less power are deprived of the means to support themselves. It characterizes the relationship of Western civilizations with the natural world, as we transform a vast array of material bodies into artifacts, despoiling creation faster than it can replenish itself.[12] These imbalances warp the matrix of created *ousia*, trading mutualistic interdependence for systems that oppress one set of material bodies for the (short-term) benefit of others.

The web of interrelations is also distorted by those who fail to acknowledge their own status as beloved creatures of God and instead spend themselves completely without accepting anything in return. Distortions can be created both by taking too much and by giving too much. If sin is going to be used as a universal signifier for that from which created beings need salvation, Christians will need to acknowledge that it manifests itself in different ways. This is not a novel suggestion.[13] Many modern theologians have stopped trying to describe all human failures under one rubric, like pride, and have instead begun examining the differences between those engaged in oppression and those suffering from it. For example, Andrew Park uses the Korean concept of *han*, "a deep unhealed wound of a victim that festers in her or him," to describe the predicament of the latter.[14] As Park notes, victims of oppression do not stand in need of forgiveness for their oppression, but rather need liberation and healing.[15] In contrast, oppressors need judgment, correction, and forgiveness.[16] While Park recognizes that most people are, in different aspects of their lives, both oppressors and oppressed, his distinction encourages Christians to recover a variety of understandings of both the human predicament and the effects of the incarnation.[17] In another approach Darby Kathleen Ray recommends that Christians avoid using many traditional definitions of sin—including disobedience, willfulness, pride, and self-love—in light of the effects these definitions can have in cases of domestic violence.[18] While hardening of the heart, betrayal of trust, and "distortion of the self's boundaries" may prove more useful, Ray notes that each needs careful nuancing when applied to the disparately situated perpetrators and survivors of domestic violence.[19]

In light of a two-*ousiai* Christology, sin might profitably be thought of as an imbalance or distortion of the relationship between "being" and "being for another" that characterizes created *ousia*. This can manifest in a failure authentically to be the creature that one is made to be, the failure to receive from others what they have to provide. It can also manifest in a failure to be for another, the failure to give to others and thus fulfill one's role within one's creaturely society. From this understanding the human predicament is characterized by sin as that distortion of created being that disregards the proper bounds of interdependence by either taking or giving more than is appropriate.

Salvation

If an imbalance between integrity and interdependence describes the thing from which creation needs saving, then salvation can be appropriately understood as that which restores created balance. This description encourages contemporary theologians to retain and expand upon the multiple metaphors Christians have traditionally used to describe salvation. Members of the human community stand in need of both forgiveness and healing, and both oppressors and the oppressed need to be freed from their captivity to unjust systems and to learn how to live in proper relationships of interdependence. The life, ministry, death, and resurrection of Jesus provide many resources for considering how the Word incarnate might bring about this forgiveness, healing, liberation, and education.

Considering salvation as the restoration of balance between the integrity and interdependence of created beings ultimately means that individual salvation cannot be separated from communal salvation. Creatures are not saved by being removed from the interdependent web of creation, but by having that web rewoven in its proper shape. Individual human beings are not saved from their creaturely condition, but experience salvation in the healing of creation. An individual decision to live in alignment with the individual integrity and communal interdependence of created *ousia* does not earn one a spot in heaven so much as it begins to remake creation here and now. Salvation involves the healing of creation, a healing that offers restoration to the community through individual actions, and offers restoration to the individual through a healed community. It will be experienced differently by people who are situated differently within the distortion—the oppressed will be lifted up while the oppressors are brought low. How the life and ministry of Jesus invites individuals and communities into this salvation remains to be developed.

Trinity

The ideas of being and being-for-another that undergird these understandings of sin and salvation also have implications for the doctrine of the Trinity and its relationship to the contingency of creation. Christians have traditionally defended divine freedom and aseity by affirming the absolute contingency of creation—that God has no need to create a universe, but does so only as an exercise of the superfluousness of divine grace. Bruce McCormack has challenged this contingency and set off a heated debate when he suggested that the divine election that occurred in the incarnation may itself constitute God as triune.[20] Van Driel argues that this would make creation intrinsic to the divine nature, contra traditional understandings of divine aseity.[21]

Divine transcendence and the limitations of human knowledge mean that developments of the doctrine of the Trinity cannot be compared to the Trinity, *in se*, and so they must be judged by their impacts on the life of faith. Before reconstructing the doctrine's foundational assumptions, it is helpful to consider the purposes those assumptions were intended to serve. The traditional Christian assertion of the contingency of creation seems intended to preserve human feelings of gratitude for the gift of this world. Similarly, assertions that God has no need of the world in order to be God seem intended to maintain the ontological distinction between God and the world while generating awe as the appropriate human response to God's absolute self-sufficiency. Unfortunately, none of these assertions have prevented the wholesale commodification and desecration of creation, the secularization of society, or the domestication of the divine in the religious imagination. Perhaps it is time to join ecofeminists and indigenous traditions in affirming a necessary relationship between God as God can be known and the world as it is. Developing a doctrine of the Trinity that understands the incarnation as the foundation, not only of created existence per se, but also of the triunity of God, might yield greater respect for the creation we experience as well as for the God we worship. Placing difference and identity at the heart of the Christian doctrine of God might yield greater tolerance of differences within our societies. These are possibilities worthy of further exploration.

ETHICAL OBLIGATIONS

A two-*ousiai* Christology invites further reconstructive work in theological anthropology, sin, salvation, and the doctrine of the Trinity. In addition to this theological reconstruction, it invites ethical reconstructive work as well. By including all of creation in the realm of God's loving care, a two-*ousiai* Christology invites Christians to consider what ethical obligations they might owe to other creatures and how they might develop the moral capacities to consider the well-being of all of creation in their decision-making processes.

When considering how to treat other creatures, humans ought to begin from a place of mutuality. This requires recognition that all of life depends on other creatures. This recognition should lead human beings to a sense of gratitude for the benefits other creatures provide. In return, humans should not simply take what is required from others while giving nothing back. Instead, we should consider how our existence might benefit other creatures as well as ourselves. This does not mean that human beings must stop using other creatures. If we tried, then we would not be able to breathe, let alone eat or drink. Furthermore, any attempt to remove ourselves from the ongoing interdependent processes of transformation would deny our reality as partakers of created *ousia*. The question is not *whether* we will use other creatures, but rather *how* we will use them.

Intra-human relations raise similar questions, and our ability to address those questions offers grounds to hope that we may be able to grapple with appropriate cross-species relations as well. Unless one withdraws from society entirely, a human being makes use of other human beings. We make use of strangers who raise our food, process it, and deliver it to shops and restaurants. We make use of merchants who sell it to us. We make use of strangers who purify our water and dispose of our waste. We make use of our friends and loved ones as well—we ask for rides, companionship, and support. Within just and loving relationships, none of these things are necessarily inappropriate. There is a form of mutuality in all of these relationships, whether it is the mutuality of remuneration for services rendered or the give-and-take of more intimate relations. It is when this mutuality is denied, when we treat others solely as resources from which we extract those things we need without giving anything in return, that ethical boundaries are crossed. The ethical question is not whether we will make use of other human beings, but how we make use of them—and what we give in return.

Following this model of ethical human relations, our relationships with other creatures need to be based on a similar understanding about what is proper use, what is abuse, and what we owe to creatures in recognition of what we receive from them. This means that we need to develop an expanded form of *phronesis*, practical wisdom that understands what is appropriate in a given situation. We seem to lack such practical wisdom when it comes to other creatures, as evidenced by the frequent failure of even those whose vocations focus on maintaining appropriate relationships with the natural world. Our attempts at environmental management have led to devastating pest outbreaks, fishery collapses, deforestation, and an extinction rate that is accelerating alarmingly. These failures indicate that we lack something necessary for creaturely *phronetic* reasoning. We lack an appropriate hermeneutic for reading the world we inhabit and our place in it. Such a hermeneutic requires that we give sustained attention to other creatures and the matrix of relationships in which they are embedded. Sallie McFague describes this as *attention epistemology*, "listening, paying attention to another, the other, in itself, for itself" and taking "with utmost seriousness the differences that separate all beings: the individual, unique site from which each is in itself and for itself."[22] The ecomimetic interpretation used to develop the definition of created *ousia* earlier provides one model for practicing such attention epistemology.

The awareness humanity once had of its dependence on other creatures, along with the attention that human beings once granted to non-human creatures, was not erased overnight. It involved the development of systems that allowed us to stop paying attention, and vested commercial interests in directing our attention elsewhere. Although cultural conditioning creates a barrier to practicing sustained attention to other creatures, making it seem nearly inconceivable that we might ever reach the noble goal of treating all creatures as moral objects in their own rights, this does not absolve us from making the attempt.[23] Human beings can begin to cultivate habits that take the value of other creatures as beloved creatures of God into account by paying attention to the webs of relationship in which they are embedded and in which they play their own unique roles. Even failed attempts to free ourselves from culturally conditioned blindness towards other creatures moves us further towards the goal, and every failed attempt to take seriously the ethical demands that other creatures place on us will make us more morally sensitive to such claims.

"IN HIM ALL THINGS HOLD TOGETHER"

A two-*ousiai* Christology invites Christians to reconsider their relationships to other creatures, reconsider their claims about the Trinity, reconstruct traditional understandings of sin and salvation in a more inclusive register, and let go of anthropocentric concerns about humanity's unique dignity within the created realm. Such a Christology grounds the created goodness of every individual being in the love that God has for it and invites each being into loving relationship with all of the beings of their communities. It claims that all of existence is grounded in and patterned after the divine willingness to be for another, which governs the shape of reality as we experience it. Furthermore, this two-*ousiai* Christology is based on traditional Christian resources, including Scripture and ecumenical decrees, and it also agrees with the best insights that modern science can provide us into the origins of life and the structure of the universe. It provides a coherent explanation of how it can be true that Jesus Christ is both divine and created while undermining all challenges that the doctrine of the incarnation supports injustices or is itself unfair.

Ultimately, the incarnation is the created expression of the divine decision to be for another, a decision that draws that other into existence. As such, it grounds the existence and integrity of the other as the one for whom God is. It also provides the shape of existence, such that the other is itself "for another" as well. Doubling and redoubling, this "being for another" offers a theological explanation for the diversity that characterizes creation. Created *ousia* is (1) being, (2) with others, (3) in a way that contributes to the existence of those others. We are incapable of extricating ourselves from the web of interrelations that govern our existence. This two-*ousiai* Christology provides a theological basis for an ethics that understands the self only in relation to other selves, as both loving and beloved. This portrait is one that we can reject only by rejecting the grounds for our existence, the balance of interdependence that can only be disturbed at our own peril.

NOTES

PREFACE

1 University of Illinois, Springfield, "Sankofa," https://www.uis.edu/africanamericanstudies/students/sankofa/.
2 See Alasdair MacIntyre's description of a living tradition as "an historically extended, socially embodied argument, and an argument precisely in part about the goods which constitute tradition." Although traditions provide the basis for practices, individuals and communities are not bound by those traditions, but can amend them. MacIntyre, "Virtues, Unity of Life and Concept of Tradition," in *After Virtue: A Study in Moral Theory*, 3rd ed. (Notre Dame: University of Notre Dame Press, 2007), 221–22.
3 In light of eco-catastrophe, Larry Rasmussen makes a similar argument that we need to do first works over, meaning we need to "reexamine everything from its onset and speak the truth as best one can." Rasmussen, *Earth-Honoring Faith: Religious Ethics in a New Key* (Oxford: Oxford University Press, 2013), 45.
4 See Sarah Coakley, *God, Sexuality, and the Self: An Essay "On the Trinity"* (Cambridge: Cambridge University Press, 2013); J. Kameron Carter, *Race: A Theological Account* (Oxford: Oxford University Press, 2008); and Elizabeth A. Johnson, *Creation and the Cross: The Mercy of God for a Planet in Peril* (Maryknoll, N.Y.: Orbis Books, 2018). This list could be expanded indefinitely because the practice of retrieving tradition is not a new development. Throughout Christian history, theologians have built upon the work of earlier theologians, from Genesis' critical retrieval of earlier narratives to Paul's

interpretation of Genesis, to Augustine's interpretation of Paul, to Luther's and Calvin's appropriation of Augustine, and beyond.

5   I would note that this caveat applies to the work at hand as well. As a woman, and therefore the member of one group historically disenfranchised by these sources, I may see the distortions that androcentrism has introduced into my tradition more clearly than do some others. This does not mean that I consider myself free from distorting influences. My citizenship, skin color, and socioeconomic class render me more shortsighted in other areas. Nevertheless, I offer here my earnest attempt to express my understanding of ultimate reality to the best of my ability, knowing full well that it is also distorted by imperfect knowledge and implicit biases.

6   As Karl Barth argues, Jesus' humanity "is binding on humanity generally," and thus a theological anthropology must begin with an understanding of Jesus' own humanity. Karl Barth, *Church Dogmatics*, vol. 3: *The Doctrine of Creation*, part 2, ed. G. W. Bromiley and T. F. Torrance (Peabody, Mass.: Hendrickson, 1995), 243. For a similar claim from the early church, see Maximus the Confessor's argument that the incarnation is the fulfillment of human destiny. Maximus, *Difficulty 41*, in *Maximus the Confessor*, ed. Andrew Louth (New York: Routledge, 1996), 157–59. Subsequent references are to this edition and reflect the modern pagination. For a modern appropriation, see Ian McFarland's explanation: "The fact that in his total obedience to God's Jesus actually succeeded in occupying the place under God that God intended for all human beings means that in Jesus, human personhood is fully and finally realized." McFarland, *Difference and Identity: A Theological Anthropology* (Cleveland: Pilgrim, 2001), 70. See also Kathryn Tanner, *Jesus, Humanity and the Trinity: A Brief Systematic Theology* (Minneapolis: Fortress, 2001), 9. For a counterexample, see Rosemary Radford Ruether's argument that Jesus provides one, but not the only, paradigm of humanity, in *Sexism and God-Talk: Toward a Feminist Theology* (1983; Boston: Beacon, 1993), 114.

1 CHRISTOLOGICAL DIVIDES

1   Pope Paul VI, "Decree on the Apostolate of the Laity," November 18, 1965, http://www.vatican.va/archive/hist_councils/ii_vatican_council/documents/vat-ii_decree_19651118_apostolicam-actuositatem_en.html.

2   Franjo Cardinal Seper, "Declaration on the Question of Admission of Women to the Ministerial Priesthood," October 15, 1976, http://www.vatican.va/roman_curia/congregations/cfaith/documents/rc_con_cfaith_doc_19761015_inter-insigniores_en.html.

3   Warner Sallman, *Head of Christ*, 1940, The Warner Salman Collection, http://www.warnersallman.com/collection/images/head-of-christ/.

Notes to Pages 2–3

4   TMP TV, "Megyn Kelly: 'Santa Is What He Is,' Which is White," YouTube video, 2:10, posted December 12, 2013, https://www.youtube.com/watch?v=7XYlJqf4dLI.
5   Southern Baptist Convention, "Resolution On Global Warming," 2007, http://www.sbc.net/resolutions/1171/on-global-warming.
6   E. Calvin Beisner, *Where Garden Meets Wilderness* (Grand Rapids: Eerdmans, 1997), 100.
7   Beisner, *Where Garden Meets Wilderness*, 53.
8   John Hick, *The Metaphor of God Incarnate: Christology in a Pluralistic Age* (Louisville: Westminster John Knox, 1993), 80.
9   See Daly's question: "If the symbol can be 'used' that way and in fact has a long history of being 'used' that way, isn't this an indication of some inherent deficiency in the symbol itself?" Mary Daly, *Beyond God the Father: Toward a Philosophy of Women's Liberation* (Boston: Beacon, 1973), 72.
10 John B. Cobb Jr., foreword to *Fidelity with Plausibility: Modest Christologies in the Twentieth Century*, by Wesley J. Wildman (Albany: State University of New York, 1998), xi.
11 Mary Daly is a prime example of a theologian who rejected continued reliance on the centrality of Jesus in light of the injustices of patriarchy. See Daly, "Beyond Christology: A World Without Models," in *Beyond God the Father*, 69–97. In contrast, Sallie McFague and Maurice Wiles, among others, address these issues by emphasizing the basic incarnational structure of Christianity as more significant than the doctrine of the incarnation as a unique event. See Sallie McFague, *The Body of God: An Ecological Theology* (Minneapolis: Augsburg Fortress, 1993), 159–96; and Maurice Wiles, "Christianity without Incarnation?" in *The Myth of God Incarnate*, ed. John Hick (Philadelphia: Westminster, 1977), 1–10.
12 For constructive responses that separate the doctrine from the sexist, racist, and ecologically destructive uses made of it, see Elizabeth A. Johnson, *She Who Is: The Mystery of God in Feminist Theological Discourse* (New York: Crossroad, 1992); James Cone, *God of the Oppressed* (New York: Seabury, 1975); Kelly Brown Douglas, *The Black Christ* (Maryknoll, N.Y.: Orbis Books, 1994); and Joseph Sittler, "Called to Unity," in *Evocations of Grace: Writings on Ecology, Theology, and Ethics*, ed. Steven Bouma-Prediger and Peter Bakken (Grand Rapids: Eerdmans, 2000), 38–50.
13 As will be discussed further in chapter 2, reformist feminist theologians like Rosemary Radford Ruether and Elizabeth A. Johnson demonstrate the flaws inherent in these assumptions.
14 Chapter 2 will take up justice challenges and how the doctrine of the incarnation can and should be separated from the abuses perpetrated in its name.
15 As Sarah Coakley notes, the incarnation is paradoxical, meaning "contrary to expectation" but not "actually 'self-contradictory' or incoherent." The

surrounding history of the ecumenical councils that formed conciliar definitions of Christology demonstrates that "the 'paradoxical' nature of the incarnation in the first sense is embraced (with greater or lesser degrees of enthusiasm), but that 'paradox' in the latter sense is vigorously warded off. The 'Definition' is propelled by an assumption of coherence, not by a glorying in incoherence." Sarah Coakley, "What Does Chalcedon Solve and What Does It Not? Some Reflections on the Status and Meaning of the Chalcedonian 'Definition,'" in *The Incarnation: An Interdisciplinary Symposium on the Incarnation of the Son of God*, ed. Stephen T. Davis, Daniel Kendall, SJ, and Gerald O'Collins, SJ (Oxford: Oxford University Press, 2002), 155.

16 See John Hick's oft-cited claim that "orthodoxy has never been able to give this idea any content. It remains a form of words without assignable meaning. For to say, without explanation, that the historical Jesus of Nazareth was also God is as devoid of meaning as to say that this circle drawn with a pencil on paper is also a square. Such a locution has to be given semantic content: and in the case of the language of incarnation every content thus far suggested has had to be repudiated." John Hick, "Jesus and the World Religions," in Hick, *Myth of God Incarnate*, 178.

17 For a description of this argument, see Timothy Pawl, *In Defense of Conciliar Christology: A Philosophical Essay* (Oxford: Oxford University Press, 2016), 75. Pawl defends conciliar Christology without challenging the definition of attributes used in the debates, ultimately concluding that the incarnation is coherent because each of the natures—divine and human—possesses the attributes ascribed to it. Idem, *In Defense of Conciliar Christology*, 153–75. This is an apt explanation of what the councils offered in setting the boundary for future christological reflection, although it does not resolve the difficulty posed. Instead, it simply highlights that the inconsistency lies at the level of the person, not the natures. The underlying question of what it means to say one person simultaneously possesses a nature that is omnipresent and a nature that is located in a particular place remains.

18 Thomas V. Morris explains this problem in some detail in *The Logic of God Incarnate* (Eugene, Ore.: Wipf and Stock, 1986), 20.

19 Morris distinguishes those who follow "the *a priorist*, Anselmian tradition, which begins with a purportedly self-evident conception of God as the greatest possible being" from those who instead "are committed to an *a posteriori*, empirical, or experiential mode of developing our idea of God." He also notes that there is a middle-ground approach that holds these two in tension, granting the *a priori* claims a presumption of truth, while also recognizing that evidence from religious experience and revelation can (and in some cases, does) overcome that presumption. Morris, *Logic of God Incarnate*, 74.

20 See Hick, *Metaphor of God Incarnate*, 73; Morris, *Logic of God Incarnate*, 19, 84.

21 Anselm, *Proslogion*, in *Basic Writings*, ed. and trans. Thomas Williams (Indianapolis: Hackett, 2007), 81.
22 Anselm, *Proslogion*, 83–84, 88.
23 Morris, *Logic of God Incarnate*, 76.
24 Chapter 3 will challenge the self-evidence of these assumptions, examining the biases that govern conclusions about what properties are great-making and what properties are not.
25 See Pawl, *In Defense of Conciliar Christology*, 91; Morris, *Logic of God Incarnate*, 19.
26 For an argument that the entire cosmos might be capable of sin, see Ryan Patrick McLaughlin, *Preservation and Protest: Theological Foundations for an Eco-Eschatological Ethics* (Minneapolis: Fortress, 2014), 332–33.Those engaged in the coherence debates, however, are not as concerned with defining precisely what human nature is as they are with determining whether the claim that Jesus was divine can be reconciled with the Gospel accounts of (and conciliar claims about) his particular life. Pawl notes that it is irrelevant whether being visible, capable of death, comprehensible, or capable of suffering can be excluded from the definition of what is essential to human nature, because Scripture and the councils assert that they are true of Jesus. See Pawl, *In Defense of Conciliar Christology*, 102–3. Human nature as a generalized condition seems to enter into the debates only at the point of determining whether Jesus was capable of sinning, based on the preconceived understanding of the divine as necessarily good. See Morris, *The Logic of God Incarnate*, 108–62.
27 Numerous theologians have defended the doctrine of the incarnation from charges of logical incoherence, offering such various responses as kenotic Christology, a two-minds proposal, and redefining the divine attributes altogether. For discussion of kenotic Christologies and their associated problems, see Pawl, *In Defense of Conciliar Christology*, 104–15, and Hick, *Metaphor of God Incarnate*, 61–79. For Morris' two-minds proposal, see Morris, *Logic of God Incarnate*, 153–62; and for a critique of that approach see Hick, *Metaphor of God Incarnate*, 47–60. For an example of process theology's revisions to classical theism, see Charles Hartshorne, *Omnipotence and Other Theological Mistakes* (Albany: State University of New York Press, 1984). For a thorough survey of recent literature on coherence debates, see "The Fundamental Problem," in Pawl, *In Defense of Conciliar Christology*, 75–96.
28 Chapter 3 will undertake this examination, shifting the emphasis from human nature to created nature, recovering the apophatic tradition that the nature of God cannot be defined by human concepts, and demonstrating that even current definitions of human nature fall short of our experience of it.
29 For a discussion of this problem, see Morris, *Logic of God Incarnate*, 170–86.
30 Vernon White discusses the psychological prejudices that undergird these assumptions, noting that "the smaller our world is, the bigger we conceive

the scope of reconciliation. So it should not surprise us if the reverse is also true, that the bigger our world, the more limited that scope of reconciliation." White, *Atonement and Incarnation: An Essay in Universalism and Particularity* (Cambridge: Cambridge University Press, 1991), 2.

31 Thomas Morris observes that "it is a bit difficult to see exactly what about distinctively modern knowledge of the scale of the universe is thought to show the absurdity of any religious beliefs based on the assumption that the earth and human beings are important to the Creator of all." Morris, *Logic of God Incarnate*, 166. The idea that the universe is too big for the doctrine of the incarnation to be plausible seems to be a category mistake based on the assumption that the divine nature, while much more powerful and much more effective than human beings, possesses limits that prevent it from operating over certain expanses of space and/or time. This view understands the divine as quantitatively superior to, but not qualitatively other than, human beings. The qualitative distinction these arguments ignore has been something Christians traditionally have wanted to affirm, and it will be discussed in further detail in chapter 3.

32 However, see Morris' argument that even non-biological exceptionality would be sufficient to secure our exceptional importance if, for instance, human beings had a unique metaphysical makeup or vocation—which scientific advances have not been able to disprove. Morris, *Logic of God Incarnate*, 166–68. Although Morris' argument is plausible, I will be arguing that Christians can affirm the universal significance of the incarnation without such an appeal to human exceptionality.

33 Although I am hesitant to engage arguments based on speculation about possible, but not empirically demonstrated, conditions in the universe such as extraterrestrial life, a metaphysical explanation of how the effects of the incarnation could be shared with all of creation, as will be offered in chapter 4, would address objections based on extraterrestrial life as well as those founded on the limitations of special revelation.

34 Related in many ways to justice challenges, plausibility challenges also lead many theologians to jettison the claim that the incarnation is a unique and unrepeatable event. For example, see John Hick, "Jesus and the World Religions," in *Myth of God Incarnate*, 167–85; and "Plural Incarnations?" in *Metaphor of God Incarnate*, 89–98. This argument is also advanced in Paul Badham and Linda Badham, *Immortality or Extinction?* (London: Macmillan, 1982).

35 Chapter 4 will offer an understanding of the unique and universal significance of the incarnation that avoids reliance on its revelatory functions for establishing that significance.

36 There are few theologians writing within the academy that propound such perspectives, but they continue to be found in popular expressions of Christianity, ranging from the Southern Baptist Convention's resolutions on global

warming and the environment to the Westboro Baptist Church's more controversial positions and demonstrations.
37 George Hunsinger refers to these as "extreme versions of Alexandrian and Antiochian Christology" that inadequately define either the divinity or humanity of Jesus. Hunsinger, "Karl Barth's Christology: Its Basic Chalcedonian Character," in *The Cambridge Companion to Karl Barth*, ed. John Webster (Cambridge: Cambridge University Press, 2002), 129.
38 Norman P. Tanner, ed., *Decrees of the Ecumenical Councils*, vol. 1, *Nicaea I–Lateran V* (London: Sheed & Ward, 1990), 5.
39 Note that Timothy Pawl defines Conciliar Christology as that "put forward by the first seven ecumenical councils of Christendom. . . . Conciliar Christology is the conjunction of all the claims made at these councils concerning the doctrine of the incarnation." Timothy Pawl, *In Defense of Conciliar Christology*, 1. Due to limitations of space and scope, this work will primarily deal with only the first four of those councils: Nicaea I (325), Constantinople I (381), Ephesus (431), and Chalcedon (451).
40 Coakley describes the boundaries set by the Council of Chalcedon as

> [F]irst ruling out three aberrant interpretations of Christ, . . . second, by providing an abstract rule of language . . . for distinguishing duality and unity in Christ, and third, presenting a "riddle" of negatives by means of which a greater (though undefined) reality may be intimated. At the same time, it recapitulates . . . the acts of salvation detailed in Nicaea and Constantinople, and then leaves us at that "boundary" . . . without any supposition that this linguistic regulation thereby explains or grasps the reality towards which it points.

Coakley, "What Does Chalcedon Solve?" 161.
41 N. Tanner, *Decrees of the Ecumenical Councils*, 5, 24.
42 See N. Tanner's discussion in *Decrees of the Ecumenical Councils*, 37–39. These Cyril-Nestorius debates will be taken up in more detail in chapter 2.
43 N. Tanner, *Decrees of the Ecumenical Councils*, 86.
44 This project resembles and yet diverges radically from a project like Pawl's, which he describes as a defense that "makes no attempt at showing Conciliar Christology to be true. . . . Rather it defeats (or, more modestly, attempts to defeat) arguments against Conciliar Christology." Pawls, *In Defense of Conciliar Christology*, 2. Instead of defending the councils, I take them as a useful, but fallible, starting point for my own constructive proposal, accepting some of their claims while setting others aside.
45 As Sarah Coakley notes, "the Chalcedonian 'Definition'—as Nicaea and Constantinople before it—*takes for granted* the achievement of salvation in Christ and then asks what must be the case about that Christ if such salvation is possible." Coakley, "What Does Chalcedon Solve?" 159. Hunsinger agrees that "the interest behind Chalcedonian Christology has always been largely

soteriological," although he argues that hermeneutical interests were also at play in the Chalcedonian definition. Hunsinger, "Karl Barth's Christology," 127–28. Even when theologians do not make this starting point explicit, concerns about how Jesus saves human beings generally govern what they find acceptable to say about Jesus Christ.

46 N. Tanner, *Decrees of the Ecumenical Councils*, 5.
47 For a survey of these resources, see Matthew Fox, *The Coming of the Cosmic Christ: The Healing of Mother Earth and the Birth of a Global Renaissance* (San Francisco: Harper & Row, 1988), 83–128.
48 Fox, *Coming of the Cosmic Christ*, 83–106, 133. Jürgen Moltmann argues that only such cosmic Christologies can adequately capture Christian claims about Jesus: "Christology can only arrive at its completion at all in a cosmic christology. All other christologies fall short and do not provide an adequate content for the experiences of the Easter witnesses with the risen Christ." Moltmann, *The Way of Jesus Christ: Christology in Messianic Dimensions* (San Francisco: HarperSanFrancisco, 1990), 278.
49 As Jaroslav Pelikan notes, this extends "to the repair of the fracture in being caused by alienation" from God, and "thus not only to guilt but also to ontology... not only restoration but consummation and perfection." Pelikan, *Jesus Through the Centuries: His Place in the History of Culture* (New Haven: Yale University Press, 1985), 68.
50 Jürgen Moltmann argues that cosmic Christology means that "Christ did not die for the reconciliation of men and women. He died for the reconciliation of the cosmos... there is no personal redemption without the redemption of nature—both human nature, and the nature of the earth with which human beings are indivisibly bound up because they live together with nature." Moltmann, *Way of Jesus Christ*, 282–83.
51 See Fox's admission that, "while the Fathers attempted to ground this theology of *Logos* and Cosmic Christ in the incarnation and earthly Jesus, they were not noticeably successful in doing so, for their platonic dualisms often failed to equip them with a love of earth and earthiness upon which a theology of the Cosmic Christ must be grounded." Fox, *Coming of the Cosmic Christ*, 109.
52 Athanasius, *On the Incarnation of the Word*, in *Christology of the Later Fathers*, ed. Edward R. Hardy (1954; Louisville: Westminster John Knox, 2006), 58–59. Subsequent citations are to this edition and reflect the modern pagination.
53 Gregory of Nyssa, *Address on Religious Instruction*, in *Christology of the Later Fathers*, ed. Hardy, 302. Subsequent references are to this edition and reflect the modern pagination.
54 Jürgen Moltmann, *The Coming of God: Christian Eschatology*, trans. Margaret Kohl (Minneapolis: Fortress, 1996), 90–95.

55 Moltmann argues that this fear of death is itself the root of sin. Moltmann, *Coming of God*, 91.

56 Humans are not the only denizens of creation, and excluding other members from the work of the incarnation undermines its universality. This does not deny its significance, per se, as the many explanations of how human salvation might affect the rest of creation demonstrate. It would, however, remove the immediacy of Christ's significance, placing human beings in the role of mediator between Christ and the rest of creation. The Christology proposed in this work affirms that the significance of the incarnation is both universal and immediate—that is, not dependent on the mediation of any other human beings.

57 Robert John Russell makes a similar argument that "we should be wary of viewing the incarnation entirely in terms of soteriology, whether or not salvation can be extended to nonhuman animals." Russell, "Jesus: The Way of All Flesh and the Proleptic Feather of Time," in *Incarnation: On the Scope and Depth of Christology*, ed. Niels Henrik Gregersen (Minneapolis: Fortress, 2015), 335.

58 Andrew Linzy makes a similar claim, arguing that "the *ousia* assumed in the incarnation is not only specifically human, it is also creaturely." Linzy, *Animal Theology* (Urbana: University of Illinois Press, 1994), 10.

59 Catherine Mowry LaCugna expresses this succinctly, claiming that "Christian theology must begin from the premise that because the mystery of God is revealed in the mystery of salvation, statements about the nature of God must be rooted in the reality of salvation history." LaCugna, *God For Us: The Trinity and Christian Life* (New York: HarperSanFrancisco, 1993), 3–4.

60 Cosmic Christologies generally accept this assumption as well. Even as they relate the work of Christ to the entire cosmos, such Christologies also affirm the unique significance of the human species in the divine plan. As Fox notes, "a theology of the Cosmic Christ is not embarrassed by the deification of humans." Fox, *Coming of the Cosmic Christ*, 109.

61 Many early theologians, including Clement of Alexandria, Irenaeus of Lyons, and Athanasius of Alexandria, asserted that the Word became human in order that human beings might become divine. See Fox, *Coming of the Cosmic Christ*, 109.

62 This is a fundamental principle of the ecological hermeneutics advanced by the Earth Bible Project: "Just as feminists have adopted an approach of reading the Bible primarily as a collection of texts with an androcentric and patriarchal orientation, so we would suspect that the Bible, being written by humans for humans, would be not only patriarchal and androcentric but also anthropocentric." Norman C. Habel, "Introducing the Earth Bible," in *Readings from the Perspective of Earth*, ed. Norman C. Habel (Sheffield: Sheffield Academic Press, 2000), 36.

63 The structure of this project follows the procedure I lay out for ecomimetic interpretation, which begins with the assumption that other creatures are theologically significant, ascertains how the tradition has used the concepts being interpreted, identifies with nonhuman creatures in redefining those concepts, and brings the new definitions into conversation with the tradition. For further discussion of this method and an example of its application to Scripture, see Rebecca Copeland, "Ecomimetic Interpretation: Ascertainment, Identification, and Dialogue in Matthew 6:24-34," *Biblical Interpretation*, forthcoming.

2 WHAT'S AN *OUSIA*?

1 "Council of Chalcedon—451," in N. Tanner, *Decrees of the Ecumenical Councils*, 86.
2 "First Council of Nicaea—325," and "Council of Chalcedon—451," in N. Tanner, *Decrees of the Ecumenical Councils*, 5, 86.
3 In his review of Aristotelian, Platonic, Stoic, and early Christian uses of the term *ousia*, Christopher Stead notes that it has no less than seven (and possibly as many as twenty-eight) different connotations. See Stead, *Divine Substance* (Oxford: Oxford University Press, 1977), 132–53.
4 As in modern taxonomies, premodern categorical terminology used species to refer to the most particular category to which a living being belonged. Unlike modern systems, however, they also used it to refer to the more particular level in a pair within the larger hierarchy of categories. That is, human beings were a species of the genus "perceptive living things," but perceptive living things was in turn a species of the genus "living things." See Paul Studtmann, "Aristotle's Categories," *The Stanford Encyclopedia of Philosophy*, ed. Edward N. Zalta (Stanford University, Summer 2014), http://plato.stanford.edu/archives/sum2014/entries/aristotle-categories/. Ancient taxonomies did use specific terms to indicate the endpoints of their systems: *infima species* indicated the most particular category that would not be subdivided further, and *genus summum* indicated the most generalized category that could not be included in another, more general, category. See *The Blackwell Dictionary of Western Philosophy*, ed. Nicholas Bunnin and Jiyuan Yu (Malden: Blackwell Publishers, 2004), s.v. "infima species" and "genus." The term *ousia* could be used synonymously with any category within the system.
5 See discussion in chapter 1. Also see Sarah Coakley, "What Does Chalcedon Solve?" 159.
6 This mixing of metaphors and commitment to divine transcendence does not mean that early theologians considered their descriptions disconnected from divine reality. In the specific context of the Chalcedonian Definition, Sarah Coakley explains that "it is often by the means of a freshly minted metaphor that one can make the most intense claims on the real," and that "the coinage

of new and striking metaphor... has more often sprung in Christian tradition from a realist commitment... than from a coyness such as Hick's about realist claims." Coakley, "What Does Chalcedon Answer?" 154.

7   See *Against Heresies* 3.18.7:

> He caused man (human nature) to cleave to and to become, one with God. For unless man had overcome the enemy of man, the enemy would not have been legitimately vanquished. And again: unless it had been God who had freely given salvation, we could never have possessed it securely. And unless man had been joined to God, he could never have become a partaker of incorruptibility. For it was incumbent upon the Mediator between God and men, by His relationship to both, to bring both to friendship and concord, and present man to God, while He revealed God to man. For, in what way could we be partaken of the adoption of sons, unless we had received from Him through the Son that fellowship which refers to Himself, unless His Word, having been made flesh, had entered into communion with us? Wherefore also He passed through every stage of life, restoring to all communion with God.... For it behoved Him who was to destroy sin, and redeem man under the power of death, that He should Himself be made that very same thing which he was, that is, man; who had been drawn by sin into bondage, but was held by death, so that sin should be destroyed by man, and man should go forth from death. For as by the disobedience of the one man who was originally moulded from virgin soil, the many were made sinners, and forfeited life; so was it necessary that, by the obedience of one man, who was originally born from a virgin, many should be justified and receive salvation.... God recapitulated in Himself the ancient formation of man, that He might kill sin, deprive death of its power, and vivify man; and therefore His works are true.

Ante-Nicene Fathers, vol. 1, ed. Alexander Roberts and James Donaldson (Grand Rapids: Christian Classics Ethereal Library, n.d.), https://www.ccel.org/ccel/schaff/anf01.ix.iv.xix.html. Subsequent references are to this edition. See also *Against Heresies* 5.1.1:

> In no other way could we have learned the things of God, unless our Master, existing as the Word, had become man. For no other being had the power of revealing to us the things of the Father, except His own proper Word. For what other person "knew the mind of the Lord," or who else "has become His counsellor?" Again, we could have learned in no other way than by seeing our Teacher, and hearing His voice with our own ears, that, having become imitators of His works as well as doers of His words, we may have communion

with Him, receiving increase from the perfect One, and from Him who is prior to all creation.

8   See Athanasius, *On the Incarnation*, 73–74:

> That it was in the power of none other to turn the corruptible to incorruption, except the Saviour himself, that had at the beginning also made all things out of nought; and that none other could create anew the likeness of God's image for men, save the image of the Father; and that none other could render the mortal immortal, save our Lord Jesus Christ, who is the very life; and that none other could teach men of the Father, and destroy the worship of idols, save the Word, that orders all things and is alone the true only begotten Son of the Father. But since it was necessary also that the debt owing from all should be paid again, for . . . it was owing that all should die . . . to this intent, after the proofs of his Godhead from his works, he next offered up his sacrifice on behalf of all, yielding his temple to death in the stead of all, in order firstly to make men quit and free of their old trespass, and further to show himself more powerful even than death, displaying his own body incorruptible as first fruits of the resurrection for all.

9   Gustaf Aulén describes three of these categories under different names, treating them as competing developments within Christian history. See Aulén, *Christus Victor: An Historical Study of the Three Main Types of the Idea of Atonement* (1931; Eugene, Ore.: Wipf & Stock, 2003). What I call martial understandings have become popularly referred to as Christus Victor models, after the title of Aulén's book, although he refers to them as classical or dramatic models. Aulén's Latin models are similar to what I term forensic, and he refers to pedagogical models as the subjective type of atonement. Although I am indebted to Aulén's work for furthering both the field's and my own clarity on these categories, I diverge from his thesis on a number of points. First, and most obviously, I find evidence for all of these models in the early church, while he argues that Latin and subjective models are later (and problematic) developments in church history. Second, I find the addition of a fourth category, therapeutic models, both necessary for discussing early Christian understandings and helpful for understanding the metaphysical commitments that shaped incarnational claims. Finally, I do not view these models as necessarily competitive with one another. My four-category typology is not exhaustive—it neglects a number of contemporary understandings of salvation. Its purpose, however, is to illuminate the christological assumptions of the early church, not describe every understanding of salvation that Christians have proposed throughout history.

10 This can be seen in pugilistic imagery like that of Irenaeus, who taught that Jesus "fought, indeed, and conquered; for He was a man fighting for the fathers, and by obedience he destroyed disobedience, because he bound the strong one and loosed the weak ones and gave salvation to His handiwork by destroying sin." *Against Heresies* 3.18.6. As noted above, martial models roughly coincide with what Aulén called classical or dramatic models, including both theories in which Jesus fought the devil in order to win humanity's freedom and those in which Jesus offered himself to the devil as a ransom in exchange for humanity's release. I group them together because in all these cases, the human predicament is understood as captivity brought about by our own failures and from which we need to be rescued.

11 Gregory of Nyssa advances a ransom model when he explains that "the enemy" chose Christ "as the ransom for those he had shut up in death's prison." Gregory of Nyssa, *Address on Religious Instruction*, 300.

12 Irenaeus, *Against Heresies* 3.18.7.

13 Forensic models relate to what Aulén called Latin models, encompassing a wide variety of substitutionary theories of atonement. The most widely influential is Anselm's substitutionary atonement based on notions of shame and honor in a feudal society, in which Jesus' gift to the Father is able to cover the dishonor done by human beings. See Anselm, *Cur Deus Homo*, in *Basic Writings*, trans. and ed. Thomas Williams (Indianapolis: Hackett, 2007), 237–326. Subsequent references are to this edition and reflect the modern pagination. Later developments cast substitutionary atonement in terms of criminal justice or economic recompense once Western society abandoned systems of shame and honor. In each of these forms, the human predicament is one of an unpayable debt incurred by sin and owed to God.

14 See Athanasius, *On the Incarnation*, 73–74; and Irenaeus, *Against Heresies* 3.18.7.

15 Pedagogical models relate to Aulén's subjective models, in which the object of work of the incarnation is neither the devil (as in martial or classic models) nor God (as in forensic or Latin models), but rather human beings, instructing them in the knowledge of God. Athanasius provides an example of pedagogical models when he describes Jesus, saying, "For like a kind teacher who cares for his disciples, if some of them cannot profit by higher subjects, comes down to their level, and teaches them at any rate by simpler courses, so also did the Word of God." Athanasius, *On the Incarnation*, 69.

16 Irenaeus, *Against Heresies* 5.1.1; and Athanasius, *On the Incarnation*, 73–74.

17 Gregory of Nyssa drew on a therapeutic model of the incarnation when he called humanity a "sick creature of the earth," used metaphors of surgery and cautery, and argued that, "when death came into contact with life, darkness with light, corruption with incorruption, the worse of these things disappeared into a state of nonexistence, to the profit of him who was freed from

these evils." Gregory of Nyssa, *Address on Religious Instruction*, 303–5. See also Brian E. Daley, SJ, "Divine Transcendence and Human Transformation: Gregory of Nyssa's Anti-Apollinarian Christology," in *Re-Thinking Gregory of Nyssa*, ed. Sarah Coakley (Malden: Blackwell, 2003), 67–76; and Vigen Guroian, "Salvation as Divine Therapy," *Theology Today* 61 (2004): 309–21.
18 Irenaeus, *Against Heresies* 3.18.7; and Athanasius, *On the Incarnation*, 73.
19 According to Irenaeus, salvation would be impossible "unless it had been God who had freely given salvation," "unless man had been joined to God," and unless "the Word had become man." *Against Heresies* 3.18.7, 5.1.1. Similarly, Athanasius credits the union of divinity with humanity in the person of Christ with the accomplishment of this work. Christ saves human beings from corruption and death "by the appropriation of his body and by the grace of the resurrection, banishing death from them like straw from the fire," renews the defaced image of God because only "the Word of God . . . in his own person . . . was the image of the Father" and "might be able to create afresh the man after the image," and fulfills the requirements of justice by "taking from our bodies one of like nature" and giving it "over to death in the stead of all . . . all being held to have died in him, the law involving the ruin of men might be undone." *On the Incarnation*, 62–63, 67.
20 Arius, *Letter to Eusebius of Nicomedia*, in *The Trinitarian Controversy*, ed. William G. Rusch (Philadelphia: Fortress, 1980), 30. Subsequent references are to this edition and reflect the modern pagination.
21 Alexander of Alexandria, *Letter to Alexander of Thessalonica*, in Rusch, *The Trinitarian Controversy*, 35. Subsequent references are to this edition and reflect the modern pagination.
22 Arius, *Letter to Eusebius*, 30.
23 Arius, *Letter to Alexander of Alexandria*, in Rusch, *The Trinitarian Controversy*, 31. Subsequent references are to this edition and reflect the modern pagination.
24 Arius, *Letter to Alexander of Alexandria*, 32.
25 Alexander of Alexandria, *Letter to Alexander of Thessalonica*, 35–36. See also *The Synodal Letter of the Council of Antioch, A.D. 325* in Rusch, *The Trinitarian Controversy*, 47.
26 Jaroslav Pelikan draws the same conclusion, asserting that "there were, according to Christian orthodoxy, only these two possibilities: either creature or Creator." Pelikan, *Jesus Through the Centuries*, 62.
27 N. Tanner, *Decrees of the Ecumenical Councils*, 5.
28 N. Tanner, *Decrees of the Ecumenical Councils*, 5.
29 Eusebius of Caesarea, *Letter to His Church*, in Rusch, *The Trinitarian Controversy*, 59.
30 This idea that God is not simply quantitatively superior to humanity, but qualitatively different from it, is also captured in the Christian teaching of

creation *ex nihilo*, which was a matter of Christian consensus from the late second century, though not defended by earlier writers like Justin Martyr. This qualitative distinction was a major point in the later theologies of both Søren Kierkegaard and Karl Barth. See Søren Kierkegaard, *Training in Christianity*, trans. Walter Lowrie (Oxford: Oxford University Press, 1941), 139; and Karl Barth, "Preface to the Second Edition," in *The Epistle to the Romans*, trans. Edwyn C. Hoskyns (Oxford: Oxford University Press, 1968), 10.

31 N. Tanner, *Decrees of the Ecumenical Councils*, 5.
32 N. Tanner, *Decrees of the Ecumenical Councils*, 5.
33 Irenaeus claimed that, "unless man had overcome the enemy of man, the enemy would not have been n legitimately vanquished," *Against Heresies* 3.18.7. Later, Gregory of Nyssa claimed that the Word had to be "clothed in some part of that flesh which he [the enemy] already held captive through sin" in order for the enemy to accept him as ransom for humanity. Gregory of Nyssa, *Address on Religious Instruction*, 300.
34 Therefore, Irenaeus explained, "it was incumbent upon the Mediator between God and man, by his relationship to both, to bring friendship and concord." *Against Heresies* 3.18.7. Anselm further develops this argument, explaining that humanity's responsibility for the trespass meant that only a human being could restore the honor previously denied.
35 As Irenaeus argued, "We could have learned in no other way than by seeing our Teacher and hearing his voice." *Against Heresies* 5.1.1. Athanasius describes the incarnation as the work of "a kind teacher" who comes down to the level of his students, and "teaches them at any rate by simpler courses." In a similar fashion "did the Word of God ... [take] to himself a body ... to the end, I say that they who think God is corporeal may from what the Lord effects by his body perceive truth, and through him recognize the Father." *On the Incarnation*, 69.
36 As Irenaeus explained, "unless man had been joined to God, he could never have become a partaker of incorruptibility." *Against Heresies* 3.18.7. Gregory of Nyssa provides further support for this argument, arguing, "how could our nature be restored if it was ... not this sick creature of earth which was united with the Divine? For a sick man cannot be healed unless the ailing part of him in particular receives the cure." *Address on Religious Instruction*, 305. Gregory of Nazianzus further developed this logic against Apollinarian arguments, arguing that "the unassumed is the unhealed, but what is united with God is also being saved." *Letter 101: The First Letter to Cledonius the Presbyter*, in *On God and Christ: The Five Theological Orations and Two Letters to Cledonius*, trans. Lionel Wickham and Frederick Williams (Crestwood, N.Y.: St. Vladimir's Seminary Press, 2002), 158. Subsequent references are to this edition and reflect the modern pagination.

37 "Council of Chalcedon—451," in N. Tanner, *Decrees of the Ecumenical Councils*, 86–87.
38 Chapter 4 will revisit this ontological account of the shared effects of the hypostatic union, although it will shift the emphasis from a shared human substance to the concept of created *ousia*, as that in which all created beings share.
39 As Pelikan notes, "it was characteristic of the Greek Christian philosophers of the fourth and fifth centuries that, by contrast with the later Christian individualism manifest especially in Western thought, they always viewed humanity and the cosmos in close proximity." Pelikan, *Jesus Through the Centuries*, 67.
40 Even those theologians who affirm the cosmic scope of the reconciliation achieved by Christ affirm such hierarchies. For example, Richard Bauckham traces effect of these hierarchies on the Christologies of Gregory the Great, Bonaventure, and Maximus the Confessor in Bauckham, "The Incarnation and the Cosmic Christ," in *Incarnation*, ed. Gregersen, 38–39.
41 Maximus, *Difficulty 41*, 157. See Torstein Tollefsen's discussion of the relationship of these divisions to the incarnation in "Saint Maximus the Confessor on Creation and Incarnation," in *Incarnation*, ed. Gregersen, 105–8.
42 Apollinaris of Laodicea, *Fragment 69*, in *The Christological Controversy*, ed. Richard A. Norris (Philadelphia: Fortress, 1980), 109. Subsequent references are to this edition and reflect the modern pagination.
43 Apollinaris of Laodicea, *Fragment 69*, 109.
44 Gregory of Nazianzus, *Letter 101*, 158.
45 Howard P. Kainz, *The Philosophy of Human Nature* (Chicago: Open Court, 2008), 4–5.
46 Aristotle, *On the Soul* 413a20–22, in *The Basic Works of Aristotle*, ed. Richard McKeon (New York: Random House, 1941), 557. Subsequent references are to this edition and reflect the original pagination.
47 Aristotle, *On the Soul*, 413a30–31.
48 Aristotle, *On the Soul*, 414b1–20.
49 Although some have interpreted the image functionally to indicate that "human beings bear God's image in that they rule over creation on God's behalf," and others have interpreted it relationally to emphasize "patterns of human mutuality," most have "interpreted the divine image *noetically* as referring to some mental capacity (e.g., reason, freedom, or self-consciousness) that elevates human beings above all other earthly creatures by virtue of the fact that they possess distinct spiritual capacities that reflect God's own transcendence of the material order." Ian A. McFarland, "Theological Anthropology," in *The Cambridge Dictionary of Christian Theology*, ed. Ian A. McFarland, David A. S. Fergusson, Karen Kilby and Iain R. Torrance (Cambridge: Cambridge University Press, 2011), 502. Christians have generally interpreted this claim exclusively, as indicating that nothing but humanity was made in the image

of God. While I have no argument that the authors of this text had anything but such an anthropocentric claim in mind, I would like to point out that the text itself does not actually say that. It does say that humanity is created in the image of God; it does not say that anything else is not.

50 Thomas Aquinas, *Summa Theologica* 1.93.2, Christian Classics Ethereal Library, n.d., https://www.ccel.org/ccel/aquinas/summa, emphasis added. Subsequent references (abbreviated as *ST*) are to this edition.

51 See Aquinas' comments on Aristotle in *ST* 1.78.2.

52 Cyril of Alexandria, *An Explanation of The Twelve Chapters*, in *Cyril of Alexandria*, ed. Norman Russell (London: Routledge, 2000), 182. Subsequent references are to this edition and reflect the modern pagination.

53 Cyril, *Against Nestorius*, in *Cyril of Alexandria*, ed. Norman Russell, 150. Subsequent references are to this edition and reflect the modern pagination.

54 Cyril, *Against Nestorius*, 142.

55 Cyril, *Against Nestorius*, 134.

56 So long as Christians maintained the universal significance of the incarnation, the converse could not be held: vegetative and animal souls were not considered ontologically distinctive, but were rather understood to be subsumed in the rational soul.

57 N. Tanner, *Decrees of the Ecumenical Councils*, 69, emphasis added.

58 N. Tanner, *Decrees of the Ecumenical Councils*, 86, emphasis added.

59 Chalcedonian Christology is often referred to as dyophysite, or "two-natures," Christology; the terms *physis* and *ousia* can be understood synonymously. However, the Chalcedonian definition retains the claims of Nicaea and Ephesus that Jesus is "consubstantial [*homoousion*] with us as regards his humanity." N. Tanner, *Decrees of the Ecumenical Councils*, 86. I refer to the logic regarding this consubstantiality as a "two-*ousiai* Christology" primarily to avoid confusion with assumptions particularly about "human nature" in English usage, although I recognize that *ousia* and *physis* are sometimes used interchangeably in ensuing christological debates.

60 Athanasius explains this in regards to human beings: "For if, out of a former normal state of nonexistence, they were called into being by the presence and loving-kindness of the Word, it followed naturally that when men were bereft of the knowledge of God . . . they should . . . be everlastingly bereft even of being; in other words, that they should be disintegrated and abide in death and corruption." Athanasius, *On the Incarnation*, 59.

61 Alexander of Alexandria, "Letter to Alexander of Thessalonica," 39.

62 Gregory of Nyssa, *Address on Religious Instruction*, 305.

63 Gregory of Nyssa, *Address on Religious Instruction*, 305–6.

64 This directly addresses injustices such as Christian patriarchy and Western colonialism that view men or those of Western culture as the mediators of salvation to women and people of non-Western cultures. An objection that one

reader has raised to this argument is that it seems to exclude the calling, election, and mediatory role of Israel. My response is twofold. Although I support readings of Scripture that show proper deference to the particularized love God demonstrates for Israel, this does not mean that Israel mediates God's love to the rest of creation. See, for example, Kendall Soulen's description of this relationship: "By electing Abraham and his seed, God has chosen in favor of genuine encounter with the human creature in his or her concreteness. The unsubstitutability of God's love for Israel is the guarantee of God's love toward all persons, elect and non-elect. The distinction between Jew and Gentile—far from indicating a limit or imperfection of God's love—testifies to God's willingness to engage all creation on the basis of divine passion." Soulen, *The God of Israel and Christian Theology* (Minneapolis: Fortress, 1996), 8. This would indicate that God's relationship to Israel is certainly revelatory of divine action in the world. If the work of the incarnation, however, proceeds through the metaphysical union of the divine with the created, rather than through the dissemination of revelation (as is suggested by conciliar logic and will be more fully developed in chapter 4), then its effects need no other mediator than the incarnate one.

65 "For the creation waits with eager longing for the revealing of the children of God; for the creation was subjected to futility, not of its own will but the will of the one who subjected it, in hope that the creation itself will be set free from its bondage to decay and will obtain the freedom of the glory of the children of God" (Rom 8:19-21).

66 It is undermined by posthumanism as well, but that is beyond the scope of this work.

67 Daniel C. Dennett, *Darwin's Dangerous Idea: Evolution and the Meanings of Life* (New York: Penguin Books, 1995), 36, 38.

68 Charles Darwin, *On the Origin of Species* (London: John Murray, 1859), 127.

69 For a summary of these debates, see Ian G. Barbour, *Religion and Science: Historical and Contemporary Issues* (San Francisco: HarperCollins, 1997), 223–25.

70 See Dennett, *Darwin's Dangerous Idea,* 85–103, for a discussion of this "Tree of Life."

71 Though serviceable in the present context, this definition may be too broad. Dennett raises this issue in regard to wolves, coyotes, and dogs, which "are considered to be different species, and yet interbreeding does occur, and—unlike mules, the offspring of horse and donkey—their offspring are not in general sterile." *Darwin's Dangerous Idea,* 45.

72 The species distinction, ostensibly based on genetic variations, can be contrasted with the nominal distinctions of breeds, which do allow for comparison to a standard to determine whether an individual can be considered of that breed or not. Breeds are categories created by human beings who define the breed by those characteristics they deem appropriate and exclude those

individuals that do not meet their definitional criteria. This model fits with premodern understandings of the relationship between species and natures, but no one today is under an illusion that the height and other limitations specified by the American Kennel Club for Chihuahuas is related to some eternally determined Form of ideal Chihuahua-ness.

73 Mark Ridley, *The Problems of Evolution* (New York: Oxford University Press, 1985), 5, cited by Dennett, *Darwin's Dangerous Idea*, 45. See also Ernst Mayr, *Systematics and the Origin of Species* (New York: Dover, 1964).

74 The work of evolutionary biologist Lynn Margulis on symbiosis has been influential on theological appropriation of these ideas. For example, see "The Creature We Are," in Rasmussen, *Earth-Honoring Faith*, 11–42.

75 Ron Sender, Shai Fuchs, and Ron Milo, "Revised Estimates for the Number of Human and Bacteria Cells in the Body," *PLoS Biology* 14.8 (2016): 1–14.

76 Xiaofei Xu, Zhujun Wang, and Xuewu Zhang. "The Human Microbiota Associated with Overall Health," *Critical Reviews in Biotechnology* 35.1 (2015): 129–40.

77 Xu, et al., "The Human Microbiota," 132–36.

78 One example of such cross-species cooperation that challenges traditional notions about the capacities of a species can be seen in the way that trees in forests make use of soil fungal networks in order to both communicate with one another and share resources. This finding challenges long-standing assumptions that plants do not have the ability to communicate and do not form any kind of social alliances. See Nic Fleming, "Plants Talk to Each Other Using an Internet of Fungus," BBC, last modified November 11, 2014, http://www.bbc.com/earth/story/20141111-plants-have-a-hidden-internet.

79 Barbour, *Religion and Science*, 195–96.

80 Barbour describes the four basic physical forces that govern material existence: "(1) the electromagnetic force responsible for light and the behavior of charged particles; (2) the weak nuclear force responsible for radioactive decay; (3) the strong nuclear force that binds protons and neutrons into nuclei; and (4) the gravitational force evident in the long-distance attraction between masses." *Religion and Science*, 196.

81 Barbour, *Religion and Science*, 215.

82 Barbour, *Religion and Science*, 233.

83 Rosemary Radford Ruether, "The Liberation of Christology from Patriarchy," *Religion and Intellectual Life* 2.3 (1985): 118. See also Ruether's discussion of the influence of Aristotelian biology on understandings of the incarnation in *Sexism and God-Talk*, 125–26.

84 As Elizabeth A. Johnson argues, "If Jesus is a man, so uncritical reasoning goes . . . then this must point to maleness as an essential characteristic of divine being itself." Johnson, *She Who Is*, 152.

85 Ruether, "The Liberation of Christology from Patriarchy," 116–17. As Ruether explains, "Women, slaves, and barbarians (as well as religious minorities,

Jews, pagans, and heretics) are the *a-logoi,* the 'mindless' ones, who are to be governed and defined by the representatives of divine *Logos."* Sexism and God-Talk, 125.

86 See Augustine, *De Trinitate,* 12.7.9–10; and Aquinas, *Summa Theologica,* 1.93.4, reply to objection 1.
87 Johnson, *She Who Is,* 152.
88 See Ruether, "The Liberation of Christology from Patriarchy," 118; and Johnson, *She Who Is,* 153.
89 Johnson, *She Who Is,* 153. See also Ruether, "The Liberation of Christology from Patriarchy," 119: "Today a Christology which elevated Jesus' maleness to ontologically necessary significance suggests that Jesus' humanity does not represent women at all. Incarnation solely into the male sex does not include women and so women are not redeemed."
90 Ruether, "The Liberation of Christology from Patriarchy," 127.
91 Johnson, *She Who Is,* 156.
92 As Mary Daly notes,

> The "particularity" of Jesus' maleness has not functioned in the same way as the "particularity" of his Semitic identity or of his youth. Non-Semites or persons over, say, thirty-three, have not been universally excluded from the priesthood on the basis that they do not belong to the same ethnic group or age group as Jesus. By contrast, the universal exclusion of women from the priesthood, and until recently from the ministry in most Protestant churches, has been justified on this basis. The functioning of the Christ image in Christianity to legitimate sexual hierarchy has frequently been blatant.

Mary Daly, *Beyond God the Father,* 79.

93 Daly would disagree with my claim here. Regarding the oppressive uses of the doctrine of the incarnation, she asks, "If the symbol can be 'used' that way and in fact has a long history of being 'used' that way, isn't this an indication of some inherent deficiency in the symbol itself?" Daly, *Beyond God the Father,* 72. To her objection, echoed by Hick, I can only respond that the oppressive use of a symbol only demonstrates the power of the symbol, not its relative goodness or evilness. Any powerful symbol can be turned to both constructive or destructive uses.

3 TRULY CREATED, TRULY CREATOR

1 See Ruether, *Sexism and God-Talk,* 12–46.
2 For example, see Maximus' understanding of the divisions of creation, in which existence is the only characteristic that human beings were thought to share with all of creation. Maximus, *Difficulty 41,* 157.

3   I refer to this as a *preliminary* definition of created *ousia* for two reasons. First, the limitations of space, reader's patience, and my own knowledge naturally constrain the number of creatures with which I will engage in developing this definition. I hope that these efforts might encourage those with greater expertise in geology, botany, biology, and cosmology to use their own areas of expertise to refine and enlarge this definition in the future. Second, because this is to my knowledge an early attempt to consider what created *ousia* might be, the concepts and language will be limited by the anthropocentric assumptions built into my own culturally constrained worldview. Only through repeated attempts to step outside of these anthropocentric assumptions can language and concepts be expanded in order to fully develop what partaking of created *ousia* entails.

4   Having ascertained what resources the tradition provides in the previous chapter, in this chapter I undertake the identification step of ecomimetic interpretation, bringing particular non-human creatures into the conversation about created *ousia*. For a further discussion of ecomimetic interpretation, see chapter 1, 100n63.

5   Divisions between the animate and inanimate are not universally recognized. A number of indigenous traditions continue to portray "inanimate" creatures such as mountains and rivers as personal beings with relationships to both humans and the divine. The concept of created *ousia* challenges the Western notion that there is a bright line dividing such entities from those that are categorized as "living."

6   Bauckham examines this approach in such early theologians as Gregory the Great, Bonaventure, and Maxiumus the Confessor. See Bauckham, "The Incarnation and the Cosmic Christ," 37–38.

7   See Bauckham, "The Incarnation and the Cosmic Christ," 38–39.

8   Bauckham notes the problem this creates, cautioning, "suppose the development of photosynthesis—the clearest defining characteristic of the plant kingdom, a property that animals do not have—were considered a transition to a new level of being.... In this case, the hierarchy of being would branch... humans ... could no longer be regarded as subsuming in themselves the defining properties of each lower level." Bauckham, "The Incarnation and the Cosmic Christ," 43.

9   Hobart M. King, "Limestone: What is Limestone and How is it Used?" http://geology.com/rocks/limestone.shtml. See also Asher Shadmon, *Stone in Israel* (Jerusalem: State of Israel Ministry of Development Natural Resource Research Organization, 1972), 28.

10 Shadmon, *Stone in Israel*, 33. By way of contrast, *chemical* limestone is formed by the precipitation of calcium carbonate from water or through evaporation

when such formations as stalactites and stalagmites are left behind. See King, "Limestone."
11   Shadmon, *Stone in Israel*, 37.
12   King, "Limestone."
13   Athanasius describes the transitory nature of all that is created *ex nihilo*, arguing that without the further gift granted only to human beings, creation possesses an "inability, by virtue of the condition of its origin, to continue in one stay." Athanasius, *On the Incarnation*, 58.
14   Matt 6:28-30; Luke 12:27-28. As a North American species, Big Bluestem would not have been the specific referent of Jesus' admonition, but it will serve the current goal of engaging an example of vegetative life.
15   Ronald J. Uchytil, "Andropogon gerardii," in U.S. Department of Agriculture, Forest Service, Rocky Mountain Research Station, Fire Sciences Laboratory, *Fire Effects Information System*, https://www.fs.fed.us/database/feis/plants/graminoid/andger/all.html.
16   Uchytil, "Andropogon gerardii."
17   Marc D. Abrams, "Effects of Burning Regime on Buried Seed Banks and Canopy Coverage in a Kansas Tallgrass Prairie," *The Southwestern Naturalist* 33.1 (1988): 65–70. See also Uchytil, "Andropogon gerardii."
18   O. J. Reichman, "Grasslands," in *Konza Prairie: A Tallgrass Natural History* (Lawrence: University Press of Kansas, 1987), 58–114.
19   "Pando, the Trembling Giant," Atlas Obscura, http://www.atlasobscura.com/places/pando-the-trembling-giant.
20   "Pando, the Trembling Giant."
21   For a list of these benefits, see Sarah Wennerberg, "Big Bluestem," *USDA/NRCS Plant Guide*, https://plants.usda.gov/plantguide/pdf/pg_ange.pdf.
22   Matthew Hall, *Plants as Persons: A Philosophical Botany* (Albany: SUNY Press, 2011), 137–56. See also Anthony Trewavas, "Aspects of Plant Intelligence," *Annals of Botany* 92 (2003): 1–20.
23   Hall, *Plants as Persons*, 144–45.
24   Trewavas, "Aspects of Plant Intelligence," 1.
25   Candice Gaukel Andrews, "The Trees are Talking," *Good Nature Travel*, September 20, 2011, http://goodnature.nathab.com/the-trees-are-talking/. See also David F. Rhoades, "Responses of Alder and Willow to Attack by Tent Caterpillars and Webworms: Evidence for Pheromonal Sensitivity of Willows," in *Plant Resistance to Insects*, ed. Paul A. Hedin (Washington, D.C.: American Chemical Society, 1983), 55–68.
26   Jane Englesiepen, "Trees Communicate: 'Mother Trees' Use Fungal Communication Systems to Preserve Forests," *Ecology*, October 8, 2012, http://www.ecology.com/2012/10/08/trees-communicate/. See also François P. Teste, Suzanne W. Simard, Daniel M. Durall, Robert D. Guy, Melanie D. Jones, and Amanda L. Schoonmaker, "Access to Mycorrhizal Networks and Roots

of Trees: Importance for Seedling Survival and Resource Transfer," *Ecology* 90.10 (2009): 2808–22.
27 Smithsonian Institution, "Numbers of Insects (Species and Individuals)," National Museum of Natural History, Entomology Section, Department of Systematic Biology, Information Sheet 18, https://www.si.edu/encyclopedia_si/nmnh/buginfo/bugnos.htm.
28 Smithsonian Institution, "Numbers of Insects (Species and Individuals)."
29 "Leaf Cutter Ants," Oakland Zoo Conservation and Education, https://www.oaklandzoo.org/animals/leaf-cutter-ant.
30 E. O. Wilson, *Biophilia* (Cambridge: Harvard University Press, 1984), 28–37.
31 Wilson, *Biophilia*, 32.
32 Wilson, *Biophilia*, 32.
33 Bárbara Monique dos Santos Reis, Aline Silva, Martín Roberto Alvarez, Tássio Brito de Oliveira, and Andre Rodrigues, "Fungal Communities in Gardens of the Leafcutter Ant Atta Cephalotes in Forest and Cabruca Agrosystems of Southern Bahia State (Brazil)," *Fungal Biology* 119.12 (2015): 1170–78.
34 As will be further discussed below, Wilson suggests that such ant colonies are better understood as superorganisms. Wilson, *Biophilia*, 36.
35 Wilson, *Biophilia*, 35.
36 What differentiates new queens from their worker sisters is unknown, but Wilson hypothesizes that the worker nurses might govern the generation of new queens through differential treatment of the eggs. Wilson, *Biophilia*, 34.
37 Wilson, *Biophilia*, 34–35.
38 "Leaf Cutter Ants."
39 Sebastian T. Meyer, Inara R. Leal, Marcelo Tabarelli, and Rainer Wirth, "Ecosystem Engineering by Leaf-cutting Ants: Nests of Atta Cephalotes Drastically Alter Forest Structure and Microclimate," *Ecological Entomology* 36.1 (2011): 14–24.
40 Meyer, et al., "Ecosystem Engineering," 14.
41 Wilson, *Biophilia*, 31.
42 Wilson, *Biophilia*, 33.
43 Charles B. Yackulic and Owen T. Lewis, "Temporal Variation in Foraging Activity and Efficiency and the Role of Hitchhiking Behaviour in the Leaf-Cutting Ant, Atta Cephalotes," *Entomologia Experimentalis et Applicata* 125.2 (2007): 125–34.
44 Garret Suen, et al., "The Genome Sequence of the Leaf-Cutter Ant Atta Cephalotes Reveals Insights into Its Obligate Symbiotic Lifestyle," *Plos Genetics* 7.2 (2011): 1–11.
45 Wilson, *Biophilia*, 36–37.
46 Wilson, *Biophilia*, 36.
47 For example, the remarkable ability of corvids (and squirrels) to recover cached foods after long periods of time, which will be discussed further below.

48 "Western Scrub-Jays (*Aphelocoma californica*)," https://www.beautyofbirds.com/westernscrubjays.html.
49 "Western Scrub-Jays (*Aphelocoma californica*)."
50 Jimmy Scott, "*Aphelocoma californica*: Western Scrub Jay," University of Michigan Animal Diversity Web, http://animaldiversity.org/accounts/Aphelocoma_californica/.
51 Scott, "*Aphelocoma californica*."
52 Scott, "*Aphelocoma californica*."
53 Scott, "*Aphelocoma californica*."
54 "Western Scrub-Jay," National Wildlife Federation, https://www.nwf.org/Educational-Resources/Wildlife-Guide/Birds/Western-Scrub-Jay.
55 Scott, "*Aphelocoma californica*."
56 Scott, "*Aphelocoma californica*."
57 Scott, "*Aphelocoma californica*."
58 Nicola S. Clayton and Anthony Dickinson, "Episodic-like Memory during Cache Recovery by Scrub Jays," *Nature* 395.6699 (1998): 272.
59 Joanna M. Dally, Nathan J. Emery, and Nicola S. Clayton, "Avian Theory of Mind and Counter Espionage by Food-Caching Western Scrub-Jays (Aphelocoma Californica)," *European Journal of Developmental Psychology* 7.1 (2010): 17–37.
60 Dally, et al., "Avian Theory," 17–37. For further discussion of alternate explanations, see discussion below.
61 In this experiment, the scrub-jays could look into one of two compartments while food was being "hidden" in one of several cups in each compartment. In the "forced-choice" compartment, all of the cups but one had lids and were therefore inaccessible, while in the "free-choice" compartment, none of the cups had lids. Because there was only one (obvious) choice in the forced-choice compartment but many in the free-choice compartment, the latter required more attention in order for the scrub-jay to select the correct cup during recovery. The Western scrub-jays showed a preference for observing the free-choice compartment during hiding, indicating that they were able to evaluate which situation required their attention and adjust their behavior accordingly. See Arii Watanabe, Uri Grodzinski, and Nicola Clayton, "Western Scrub-Jays Allocate Longer Observation Time to More Valuable Information," *Animal Cognition* 17.4 (2014): 859–67.
62 See Kierkegaard, *Training in Christianity*, 139; and Barth, "The Preface to the Second Edition," in *The Epistle to the Romans*, 10.
63 Elske van der Vaart, Rineke Verbrugge, and Charlotte K. Hemelrijk, "Corvid Re-Caching without 'Theory of Mind': A Model," *PLOS ONE* 7.3 (2012): 1–8.
64 James M. Thom and Nicola S. Clayton, "Re-Caching by Western Scrub-Jays (*Aphelocoma Californica*) Cannot Be Attributed to Stress," *PLOS ONE* 8.1 (2013): 1–4.
65 As ethologist Frans de Waal argues,

That we can't compete with squirrels and nutcrackers [on retrieving caches]—I even forget where I parked my car—is irrelevant, since our species does not need this kind of memory for survival.... There are lots of wonderful cognitive adaptations out there that we don't have or need. *That is why ranking cognition on a single dimension is a pointless exercise. Cognitive evolution is marked by many peaks of specialization.* The ecology of each species is key.

See *Are We Smart Enough to Know How Smart Animals Are?* (New York: W. W. Norton, 2016), 12 (emphasis added).

66 Some readers have raised the issue that this examination excludes immaterial creatures—namely, angels. Although the tradition has waxed eloquent on the precise nature of angels, I know of no evidence that would exempt them from this definition of created *ousia*. Scripture describes angels as perceptible beings that appear to, eat with, speak with, and possibly, depending on one's interpretation of Gen 6:1-5, even copulate with human beings (see Gen 18:2-15, as well as Luke 1:26-38 and 2:8-15). The tradition has also held that some angels have "fallen," or been tempted away from their divinely ordained purposes (see Isa 14:12-14 and Luke 10:18). This would indicate that they also influence and are influenced by other members of creation. Therefore, unless someone produces evidence that angels are not engaged in such mutually transformative relationships, I see no reason to modify this definition or belabor the point with further speculation on the possible nature of angelic beings.

67 James Lovelock, "Gaia: The Living Earth," *Nature* 426.6968 (2003): 769-70. This resonates with Niels Henrik Gregersen's critique of what he calls a dermal ontology, arguing that "there are no fixed borderlines between a human being and his or her surroundings, in contrast to a 'dermal metaphysics,' which assumes that the skin of individual bodies delineates the ultimate ontological ground (as in Aristotle's substance metaphysics)." Gregersen, "Deep Incarnation and *Kenosis*: In, With, and As: A Response to Ted Peters," *Dialog* 52.3 (2013): 259.

68 Logically, it would appear that there will be limits—that there are some material bodies that are the smallest components of reality that are not made up of any other material bodies, and that there is one comprehensive category, such as all material existence, that is not part of any larger material body. Even these bodies, however, change through their relationships with other material bodies, whether those bodies are perceived as external or internal to them.

69 Chapter 4 will take up in more detail how this "something" might be understood as both a substance and a relationship, depending upon the fundamental assumptions of the metaphysics at play.

70 Chapter 4 will explore the way the incarnation affects all of creation in more detail.

71 With the possible exception of peccability, the "ability" to sin. Theological arguments for the exceptionality of human beings, however, have not isolated this attribute as what makes human beings unique, focusing instead on our freedom. If plants and other animals possess a similar ability to do or not do a thing, which they do seem to, then this capacity is also not unique to human nature. Other creatures would also possess the ability to deviate from some divine plan for their existences, and would therefore be peccable, as well.

72 For a discussion of various cosmological and ontological arguments, see David Braine, "Cosmological arguments" and Peter van Inwagen, "Ontological Arguments," in *Philosophy of Religion: A Guide to the Subject*, ed. Brian Davies (Washington, D.C.: Georgetown University Press, 1998), 42–58.

73 Dionysius the Areopagite, *On the Divine Names and the Mystical Theology*, trans. C. E. Rolt (New York: Macmillan, 1957). Subsequent references are to this edition and reflect the modern pagination.

74 Pseudo-Dionysius denies God even those predicates human beings value positively, including soul, mind, imagination, reason, understanding, unity, light, and truth, "for while applying affirmations or negations to those orders of being that come next to It, we apply not unto It either affirmation or negation, inasmuch as It transcends all affirmation by being the perfect and unique Cause of all things, and transcends all negation by the pre-eminence of Its simple and absolute nature—free from every limitation and beyond them all." Dionysius the Areopagite, *On The Divine Names*, 200–201.

75 As Denys Turner explains, this involves both "affirmation and negation . . . the cataphatic and the apophatic. We must both affirm and deny all things of God; and then we must negate the contradiction between the affirmed and the denied." Turner, *The Darkness of God: Negativity in Christian Mysticism* (Cambridge: Cambridge University Press, 1995), 22.

76 Turner, *The Darkness of God*, 23. This echoes Gregory of Nyssa's argument that evil alone is unworthy of God. *Address on Religious Instruction*, 305.

77 As Turner argues, the power of this illusion is what spurs Dionysius to insist on making impious, inappropriate affirmations about the divine: "the multiplicity of vulgar images . . . because they lack any plausibility as comprehensive or appropriate names, paradoxically have a more uplifting efficacy." *The Darkness of God*, 24–25.

78 Anselm attributes some of the inability of the created intellect to grasp God to the distortions of sin, asserting that "the sinful senses of my soul have grown rigid and dull, and have been obstructed by their long listlessness." Anselm, *Proslogium*, in *St. Anselm: Proslogium; Monologium; An Appendix in Behalf of the Fool by Gaunilon; and Cur Deus Homo*, ed. and trans. Sidney Norton Deane (Eugene, Ore.: Wipf & Stock, 2003), 23. Subsequent references (for *Proslogium* and *Monologium*) are to this edition and reflect the modern pagination. Not only sin, but the natural limits of creaturely finitude prevent human beings

from comprehending God as far as God can reveal God's self. As Aquinas explained, God knows God's self infinitely, but no created intellect can know in this infinite manner and therefore revelation is a higher form of knowledge than natural reason. *ST* 1.12.7 and 1.12.13. But see the discussion of Duns Scotus below for a more optimistic view of human capacities.

79 For example, Aquinas argued that God's existence and God's status as first cause could be demonstrated through reason without appeal to supernatural revelation. *ST* 1.12.12.

80 See Anselm's prologue to the *Proslogium*: "I began to ask myself whether there might be found a single argument which would require no other for its proof than itself alone, and alone would suffice to demonstrate that God truly exists." Anselm, *Proslogium*, 2. See also Thomas Aquinas on demonstrations of God's existence, *ST* 1.2.3.

81 Anselm, *Monologium*, 61–64, and *Proslogium*, 22. For further discussion of Anselm's conception of God, see chapter 3, pp. 51ff. Although Aquinas bases his descriptions of God on a number of different arguments, he also appeals to the idea that God is that "something which is truest, something best, something noblest, and consequently something which is uttermost being," and therefore "to all beings the cause of their being, goodness, and every other perfection." *ST* 1.1.3. Duns Scotus draws on Anselm's logic in developing his idea of pure or unqualified perfection—which William E. Mann helpfully describes as a perfection that is "multiply realizable" and "has no intrinsic limitation and does not, in itself, confer an intrinsic limitation on its possessor." William E. Mann, "Duns Scotus on Natural and Supernatural Knowledge of God," in *The Cambridge Companion to Duns Scotus*, ed. Thomas Williams (Cambridge: Cambridge University Press, 2006), 247.

82 I have previously written on this line of commercials. See Copeland, "It's Not Complicated," *Placing American Religions*, March 2013, https://scholarblogs.emory.edu/placingamericanreligions/author/rlcopel/. For the commercial see "AT&T TV Commercial—It's Not Complicated 'Grandma,'" YouTube video, 0:30, posted by "H. Jay Yun" on January 3, 2013, https://www.youtube.com/watch?v=fG3_kC5Gxv0.

83 Although Scotus and others tried to avoid this problem by seeking pure perfections that were greater for any and every being to possess, their assessments relied on anthropocentric preferences in determining that it would be better for a thing to cease to be what it was in order to possess such attributes as living or wise. See Peter King, "Scotus on Metaphysics," in *Cambridge Companion to Duns Scotus*, ed. Williams, 26.

84 Moltmann expands this connection to ecological abuse, arguing that "the aggressive ethic of the modern world reflects the mentality of unreconciled human beings and their nihilistic dreams of almighty power." Moltmann, *The Way of Jesus Christ*, 307.

85   Aquinas, *ST* 1.13.2-5.
86   Such names "belong properly to God, and more properly to Him than they belong to creatures.... But as regards their mode of signification, they do not properly and strictly apply to God; for their mode of signification applies to creatures." Aquinas, *ST* 1.13.3.
87   Aquinas, *ST* I.13.5.
88   In contrast, negative names (like omnipresent or omnipotent) that deny the divine possesses creaturely limitations, "manifestly do not at all signify His substance, but rather express the distance of the creature from Him ... *or rather, the relation of creatures to Himself.*" Aquinas, *ST* 1.13.2 (emphasis added).
89   William Mann, "Duns Scotus on Natural and Supernatural Knowledge of God," 246.
90   Mann, "Duns Scotus on Natural and Supernatural Knowledge of God," 246.
91   See Mann, "Duns Scotus on Natural and Supernatural Knowledge of God," 244–46.
92   See Mann's discussion of Ord. I, d. 3, pars I, q. I., in "Duns Scotus on Natural and Supernatural Knowledge of God," 240 and 246.
93   King, "Scotus on Metaphysics," 27–28.
94   Mann, "Duns Scotus," 244.
95   Anselm, *Monologium*, 83–84, 88.
96   Scotus denies that such "negative" attributes are, in fact, negative. See Mann's discussion of Maimonides and Scotus, "Duns Scotus," 240–42.
97   Classical theism does not make this argument explicitly, rather affirming the goodness but imperfection of created reality. The way that classical theists deploy the divine attributes, however, misuses apophatic approaches to divine transcendence and treats attributes as either good, and therefore applicable to the divine, or not, and therefore inappropriate to attach to the divine.
98   This recognition of the difficulties divine transcendence creates for describing God underlies Aquinas' analogical approach to naming, discussed above. See Aquinas, *ST* 1.13. Scotus also recognizes the distinction between knowing something about a concept and comprehending it fully, and agrees that naming by finite creatures does not necessarily indicate comprehension of the thing named. See Dominik Perler, "Duns Scotus's Philosophy of Language," in *Cambridge Companion to Duns Scotus*, ed. Williams, 178–80.
99   Aquinas, *ST* 1.12.12.
100 As Cobb and Griffin explain, "to be actual is to be a process. Anything that is not a process is an abstraction from process, not a full-fledged actuality." They further note how affirmation of process brings their approach into conflict with *a priori* approaches: "Since the world as we experience it is a place of process, of change, of becoming, of growth and decay, the contrary notion that what is actual or fully real is beyond change leads to a devaluation of life

in the world." John B. Cobb Jr. and David Ray Griffin, *Process Theology: An Introductory Exposition* (Louisville: Westminster John Knox, 1976), 14.

101 If it did, then it would seem that God cares for the quaking aspen more than for human beings, and for mountains more than either. Human hierarchies of value reflect anthropocentric biases in their inconsistent treatment of these issues.

102 Even more anthropocentric approaches to theology find this diversity to be a positive aspect of created reality. See Aquinas' argument that "He brought things into being in order that His goodness might be communicated to creatures, and be represented by them; and because His goodness could not be adequately represented by one creature alone, He produced many and diverse creatures, that what was wanting to one in the representation of the divine goodness might be supplied by another." Aquinas, *ST* 1.47.1.

103 Again, while the tradition holds that angels are not born and do not die, and so this description might not be applicable to such beings, they are still transformed and transforming in their mutual interactions with other members of creation.

104 Following Aquinas' logic of analogical predication, one *could* argue that the created goodness of mutability, diversity, transience, and mutuality finds its source in the divine interdependence and multiplicity of the Trinity. However, I am not making that argument here. I am simply arguing that claims based on the supposed self-evidence of "great-making attributes" should not be granted the deference they have traditionally received.

105 As Kathryn Tanner explains, divine transcendence is "a grammatical remark about theological language: it signals a general linguistic disturbance, *the failure of all predicative attribution*, in language about God." Kathryn Tanner, "Creation Ex Nihilo as Mixed Metaphor," *Modern Theology* 29.2 (2013): 138 (emphasis added).

106 Tanner goes on to argue that "when one affirms that God is immaterial one is not denying that God has bodily existence." K. Tanner, "Creation Ex Nihilo," 139. Neither corporeality nor incorporeality can be literally (i.e., univocally) predicated of the divine.

107 This is not an exhaustive list of every challenge that has been raised, and I will make no attempt to intervene in every aspect of the coherence debates. These do represent three significant topics, however, and by addressing them I intend to model how a two-*ousiai* Christology might also respond to other challenges.

108 Anselm, *Proslogion*, 90.

109 Anselm, *Proslogion*, 89.

110 Anselm, *Proslogion*, 91.

111 Aquinas, *ST* 1.3.7, 1.4.1, 1.9.1.

112 For example, Gen 6:5-6 describes God as "sorry that he had made humankind on the earth," while Jas 4:8 instructs, "Draw near to God, and he will draw

near to you." Experiencing regret and drawing near to human beings are both indicative of some form of change.
113 Stephen T. Davis, *Logic and the Nature of God* (Grand Rapids: Eerdmans, 1983), 48.
114 Davis, *Logic and the Nature of God*, 48. This supports the insight gleaned from an examination of created *ousia* that it is appropriate to attribute an unchanging faithfulness to God. For further discussion of the trait of divine immutability, see Norman Kretzman, "Omniscience and Immutability," in *Philosophy of Religion*, ed. William Rowe and William Wainwright (New York: Harcourt, Brace, Jovanovich, 1973), 60–70; W. Norris Clarke, "A New Look at the Immutability of God," in *God: Knowable and Unknowable*, ed. Robert J. Roth (New York: Fordham University Press, 1973), 43–72; P. T. Geach, *Logic Matters* (Oxford: Blackwell, 1972).
115 Pawl, *In Defense of Conciliar Christology*, 107–8. See also Morris, *The Logic of God Incarnate*, 95–96.
116 N. Tanner, *Decrees of the Ecumenical Councils*, 5. Cited in Pawl, *In Defense of Conciliar Christology*, 16, 98–104.
117 The Council of Chalcedon "accepted the synodical letters of the blessed Cyril... to Nestorius and to the Orientals," referring to Cyril's *Second Letter to Nestorius* and *Letter to John of Antioch*; see N. Tanner, *Decrees of the Ecumenical Councils*, 85. However, Pawl notes that there is dispute as to whether the *Third Letter to Nestorius* was accepted at Chalcedon or the Second Council of Constantinople. Nevertheless, he argues that the consensus view is that this letter is part of "Conciliar Christology." Pawl, *In Defense of Conciliar Christology*, 12–13.
118 N. Tanner, *Decrees of the Ecumenical Councils*, 51. Cited in Pawl, *In Defense of Conciliar Christology*, 108, although Pawl begins his citation with the second sentence included in my quotation.
119 N. Tanner, *Decrees of the Ecumenical Councils*, 72. Cited in Pawl, *In Defense of Conciliar Christology*, 109, although Pawl ends his citation with the parenthetical.
120 N. Tanner, *Decrees of the Ecumenical Councils*, 45.
121 Of course, it would also be true that human nature outlasts its individual instantiations. But human beings have not always existed, they do not exist everywhere, and there is no guarantee that they will continue to exist as long as the rest of creation does. So human nature could not be considered immortal, everlasting, or omnipresent in the same way that created *ousia* can be.
122 This can be understood analogously to Wilson's description of the *A. cephalotes* colony as a superorganism: each ant is located in one specific place, but the colony is present wherever any member is. Wilson, *Biophilia*, 36. Similarly, created *ousia* is present wherever there is an existent created being. This would include any immaterial realities that could be considered a part of creation as well.

4 AND GOD BECAME A CREATURE

1 The Council of Nicaea (325) asserts that it was "for us humans and for our salvation he came down and became incarnate." The First Council of Constantinople (381), the Council of Ephesus (431), and the Council of Chalcedon (451) all agree that the purpose of the incarnation was "for us humans and for our salvation." See N. Tanner, *Decrees of the Ecumenical Councils*, 5, 24, 69, 86–87.

2 Although I am indebted to Edwin Christian van Driel's detailed examination of the differences between infralapsarian Christologies ("the divine will to become incarnate logically follows ... the divine will to allow sin") and supralapsarian ones ("the divine will to become incarnate logically precedes ... the divine will to allow sin"), a distinction between salvation Christologies (the incarnation occurred to save humanity—or creation—from some deficiency) and creation ones (the incarnation provides the ground for creation to exist in the first place) is more relevant to the current argument. See van Driel, *Incarnation Anyway: Arguments for Supralapsarian Christology* (Oxford: Oxford University Press, 2008), 4.

3 Some supralapsarian salvation Christologies hold that the incarnation is necessary for human beings to achieve their destined communion with the divine. See van Driel's discussion of Isaak Dorner and his own proposal in *Incarnation Anyway*, 33–61, 145–70. Although such proposals do not require a repudiation of the goodness of creation, they do seem to limit the significance of the incarnation to a particularly human understanding of relationship.

4 For example, John Cobb notes that "many thoughtful believers are clear that they do not want to continue to make assertions about Jesus Christ that are anti-Jewish or sexist.... Many want to avoid, in general, language that appears to belittle the faith of people in other religious communities." Cobb, foreword to *Fidelity with Plausibility*, xi.

5 Creation Christologies affirm the universal significance of the incarnation while acknowledging that not all members of creation can be included in the human predicament, nor need redemption from sin in the way that Christians have traditionally held human beings do. As Holmes Rolston III argues, "Human sin did not throw nature out of joint; nature does not need to be redeemed on that account." Rolston, "Does Nature Need to Be Redeemed?" *Zygon* 29 (1994): 207.

6 Even those who would extend this salvation to other creatures are often influenced by anthropocentric assumptions. See, for example, the emphasis on life, resurrection, and immortality (which marginalizes consideration of inanimate creation) in Jürgen Moltmann, "Is God Incarnate in All That Is?" in *Incarnation*, ed. Gregersen, 119–31; and Denis Edwards, "Incarnation and the Natural World: Explorations in the Tradition of Athanasius," in *Incarnation*, ed. Gregersen, 157–76.

7   For instance, in one brief passage, Athanasius invokes no fewer than five different understandings of the salvation the Word brings (incorruptibility, restoration of the image of God, immortality, true knowledge of God, and pardon for sin):

> That it was in the power of none other to turn the corruptible to incorruption, except the Saviour himself, that had at the beginning also made all things out of nought; and that none other could create anew the likeness of God's image for men, save the image of the Father; and that none other could render the mortal immortal, save our Lord Jesus Christ, who is the very life; and that none other could teach men of the Father, and destroy the worship of idols, save the Word, that orders all things and is alone the true only begotten Son of the Father. But since it was necessary also that the debt owing from all should be paid again, for . . . it was owing that all should die . . . to this intent, after the proofs of his Godhead from his works, he next offered up his sacrifice on behalf of all, yielding his temple to death in the stead of all, in order firstly to make men quit and free of their old trespass, and further to show himself more powerful even than death, displaying his own body incorruptible as first fruits of the resurrection for all.

On the Incarnation, 73–74.

8   The one exception to this problem would seem to be understandings of salvation as forgiveness. Nothing in lived experience contradicts the notion that God has forgiven human beings their trespasses.

9   Athanasius provides a helpful summary of this argument in *On the Incarnation*, 58–59.

10 Holmes Rolston III points out this absurdity with his question, "Dust devils are transient; transfigured in Jesus, do they become immortal? Even rocks are transient on geological scales, stars on cosmic scales. Is all transience transfigured to permanence in the great redemption?" Rolston, "Divine Presence: Causal, Cybernetic, Caring, Cruciform," in *Incarnation*, ed. Gregersen, 262.

11 Athanasius again provides an example of this approach, arguing that God originally gifted humanity with the means to know God, but that once human beings turned towards contemplation of themselves instead, God sent the Word as a teacher. *On the Incarnation*, 65–69.

12 John Hick highlights the theological effect of this belief, "never formulated as an official dogma but nevertheless implicit within the eighteenth- and nineteenth-century Protestant missionary expansion," that there is "no salvation outside Christianity," arguing that "this differs from other elements of Christian belief in that it is not only a statement about the potential relationship of Christians to God but at the same time about the *actual* relationship of non-Christians to God. It says that the latter, in virtue of being non-Christians,

lack salvation." Hick, *The Metaphor of God Incarnate*, 147. In an increasingly secular and pluralistic world, fewer Christians are willing to accept that their friends, family, and neighbors are excluded from salvation for reasons that are frequently beyond their control.

13. First Peter attempts to address this issue by arguing that Jesus brought his message to those who predeceased him, claiming, "For Christ also suffered for sins once for all, the righteous for the unrighteous, in order to bring you to God. He was put to death in the flesh, *in which also he went and made a proclamation to the spirits in prison,* who in former times did not obey" (3:18-20, emphasis added).

14. The enslavement of Africans and their descendants was a legally protected right in North America for more than two hundred years. Defenders of this practice such as Jefferson Davis argued that it benefited those enslaved because they were "enlightened by the rays of Christianity." Brian Palmer and Seth Freed Wessler, "The Costs of the Confederacy," *Smithsonian Magazine*, December 2018, https://www.smithsonianmag.com/history/costs-confederacy-special-report-180970731/. According to this logic, those who kidnapped African people and brought them to America were actually saving the immortal souls of those enslaved by bringing them to a place where they would learn about Christ's life. Similarly, colonial expansion was frequently justified by aligning itself with missionary expansion that brought Christianity to the farthest reaches of the globe.

15. This concern has led some theologians to propose the possibility of multiple incarnations, perhaps one for each planet hosting sentient life, or even one for each species. For a discussion of this trajectory, see Hick, *The Metaphor of God Incarnate*, 89–90. This argument is also advanced in Badham and Badham, *Immortality or Extinction?*

16. Alternatively, see Ryan Patrick McLaughlin's argument that the entire cosmos does indeed sin, as it strayed from its divinely appointed course from the very beginning. McLaughlin, *Preservation and Protest*, 332–33.

17. Romans 8:19-23: "For the creation waits with eager longing for the revealing of the children of God; for the creation was subjected to futility, not of its own will but by the will of the one who subjected it, in hope that the creation itself will be set free from its bondage to decay and will obtain the freedom of the glory of the children of God. We know that the whole creation has been groaning in labor pains until now; and not only the creation, but we ourselves, who have the first fruits of the Spirit, groan inwardly while we wait for adoption, the redemption of our bodies."

18. For modern examples of such approaches, again see van Driel's discussion of Isaak Dorner and his own proposal in *Incarnation Anyway*, 33–61, 145–70.

19. This perspective finds scriptural support in the groaning of creation that was "subjected to futility not by its own will" in Rom 8:19-23.

20 John Polkinghorne notes the importance of allowing for the particularity of God's relationship to different creatures: "The form of divine relationship to creatures must surely always be that which is fully appropriate to the individual natures of the creatures involved.... We should not think that a single concept could properly describe the divine relationship to stars, amoebas, rabbits, and human beings." Polkinghorne, "Afterword: Reservations," in *Incarnation*, ed. Gregersen, 357.

21 See M. C. Steenberg, *Irenaeus on Creation: The Cosmic Christ and the Saga of Redemption* (Boston: Brill, 2008). See also Richard Bauckham's discussion of the cosmic Christ in Bonaventure and Maximus the Confessor, "The Incarnation and the Cosmic Christ," 38–39.

22 Two early examples of this move include Pierre Teilhard de Chardin and Joseph Sittler, although it can be found in later ecotheologians as well. See Teilhard de Chardin, *Science and Christ* (New York: Harper & Row, 1968), and *Christianity and Evolution* (New York: Harcourt, Brace, Jovanovich, 1974). See also Sittler, "Called to Unity," 46. For more recent developments and application, see J. A. Lyons, *The Cosmic Christ in Origen and Teilhard de Chardin* (Oxford: Oxford University Press, 1982); Fox, *The Coming of the Cosmic Christ*; H. Paul Santmire, "Toward a Cosmic Christology: A Kerygmatic Proposal," *Theology and Science* 9.3 (2011): 287–305; and Moltmann, "The Cosmic Christ," in Moltmann, *The Way of Jesus Christ*, 274–312.

23 Sittler, "Called to Unity," 38–50.

24 Moltmann, "The Cosmic Christ," in *The Way of Jesus Christ*, 274–312.

25 The term "deep incarnation" was coined by Niels Henrik Gregersen to describe the idea that "God has not only assumed human nature in general, but also a scorned social being and a human-animal body, at once vibrant and vital and yet vulnerable to decease and decay. In this sense the cross of Christ becomes a microcosm of the whole macrocosm of evolutionary history." Gregersen, "The Cross of Christ in an Evolutionary World," *Dialog* 40.3 (2001): 193.

26 As Gregersen explains,

> "Deep incarnation" is the view that God's own Logos (Wisdom and Word) was made flesh in Jesus the Christ in such a comprehensive manner that God, by assuming the particular life story of Jesus the Jew from Nazareth, also conjoined the material conditions of creaturely existence ("all flesh"), shared and ennobled the fate of all biological life forms ("grass" and "lilies"), and experienced the pains of sensitive creatures ("sparrows" and "foxes") from within. Deep incarnation thus presupposes a radical embodiment that reaches into the roots (*radices*) of material and biological existence as well as into the darker sides of creation: the *tenebrae creationis*.

Gregersen, "The Extended Body of Christ," in *Incarnation*, ed. Gregersen, 225–26.

27 See Elizabeth A. Johnson, "Jesus and the Cosmos: Soundings in Deep Incarnation," in *Incarnation*, ed. Gregersen, 148–50. See also Johnson, *Ask the Beasts: Darwin and the Love of God* (London: Bloomsbury, 2014), 207–10; and *Creation and the Cross*, 187–94.

28 Christopher Southgate, "Does God's Care Make Any Difference? Theological Reflection on the Suffering of God's Creatures," in *Christian Faith and the Earth: Current Paths and Emerging Horizons in Ecotheology*, ed. Ernst M. Conradie, Sigured Bergmann, Celia Deane-Drummond and Denis Edwards (London: Bloomsbury, 2014), 97–114; Southgate, "Depth, Sign and Destiny," in *Incarnation*, ed. Gregersen, 208–10; and Southgate, *The Groaning of Creation: God, Evolution and the Problem of Evil* (Louisville: Westminster John Knox, 2008). See also Johnson, *Creation and the Cross*, 189–94.

29 Gregersen, "The Cross of Christ in an Evolutionary World," 198–99.

30 Gregersen, "Deep Incarnation and *Kenosis*," 259.

31 Ted Peters raises the lack of such a conceptual framework in his critique of deep incarnation, asking, "Just *how* is Christ really present?" and arguing that deep incarnation falls short of offering any explanation of this claim. See Ted Peters, "Happy Danes and Deep Incarnation," *Dialog* 52.3 (2013), 244, 249–50. Although I agree with Gregersen that attempting to offer a complete explanation of either the incarnation or the method by which God works in the world "would be presumptuous," I also think that a two-*ousiai* Christology has something to contribute to this conversation. Gregersen, "Deep Incarnation and *Kenosis*," 251. Gregersen avoids the implications of deep incarnation for conciliar Christology and vice versa, noting that "since the 1960's christological thinking has suggested that we may construct a Christology with the same scope and fulfilling similar functions as the patristic Christology without resorting to the built-in metaphysics of the Chalcedonian formula." Gregersen, "The Cross of Christ in an Evolutionary World," 201. Nevertheless, as will be discussed more fully below, claims like "the incarnation of God in Christ can be understood as a radical or 'deep incarnation,' that is, an incarnation into the very tissue of biological existence, and system of nature" are more fully supported through the revised metaphysic of a two-*ousiai* Christology, in which created *ousia* is the very tissue of not only biological existence, but all of creation. Gregersen, "The Cross of Christ in an Evolutionary World," 205.

32 For instance, see Barth's claim that "that other to which God stands in relationship . . . *is not simply and directly the created world as such*. There is, too, a relationship of God to the world," but "*this history has no independent signification*." Karl Barth, *Church Dogmatics*, vol. 2, *The Doctrine of God*, part 2, ed. G. W. Bromiley and T. F. Torrance (Peabody, Mass.: Hendrickson, 1995), §32.I, 7–8 (emphasis added). Subsequent references are to this edition. Barth's anthropocentrism

derives partly from the anthropocentric trajectory of protestant theology and partly from a reaction to some Christians' use of natural theology to support Nazism. See John Webster, *Barth* (London: Continuum, 2000), 112; and H. Paul Santmire and John B. Cobb, Jr., "The World of Nature According to the Protestant Tradition," in *The Oxford Handbook of Religion and Ecology*, ed. Roger S. Gottlieb (Oxford: Oxford University Press, 2010), 133. In contrast, see Geoff Thompson's argument that Barth's work is itself a critique of a certain kind of anthropocentrism and "is not an insignificant resource for Christian theologians seeking to engage" environmental ethics. Thompson, "'Remaining Loyal to the Earth': Humanity, God's Other Creatures and the Bible in Karl Barth," in *Ecological Hermeneutics: Biblical, Historical and Theological Perspectives*, ed. David G. Horrell, Cherryl Hunt, Christopher Southgate and Francesca Stavrakopoulou (New York: T&T Clark, 2010), 181–95.

33 Barth argues that God "had no need of creation. He might well have been satisfied with the inner glory of His threefold being.... The fact that He is not satisfied, but that His inner glory overflows and becomes outward, the fact that He wills the creation ... is grace, sovereign grace, a condescension inconceivably tender." Barth, *CD* II.2, 121. Without wading too deeply into troubled waters, there may be reason to question this traditional claim if Bruce McCormack is correct in positing that for Barth, "the triunity of God is a function of the divine election ... it is God's act of determining himself to be God for us in Jesus Christ which constitutes God as triune." McCormack, "Seek God Where He May Be Found: A Response to Edwin Christian van Driel," *Scottish Journal of Theology* 60.1 (2007): 67. Edwin Christian van Driel argues that McCormack's reading would deny the contingency of creation, observing that "incarnation implies creation.... Therefore, if election is essential to God, then so is creation." Van Driel, "Karl Barth on the Eternal Existence of Jesus Christ," *Scottish Journal of Theology* 60.1 (2007): 54. Without addressing this critique directly, McCormack affirms that

> "God would be God without us" is a true statement and one whose truth must be upheld at all costs if God's grace is to be truly gracious. But it is also a statement which stands at the very limits of what human beings ought to say about God. If we were to go further and seek to specify precisely what God would be without us—as occurs, for example, when Molnar says that God would still be triune without us—then we would make ourselves guilty of the abstract metaphysical speculation which was the bane of early church theology.

McCormack, "Seek God Where He May Be Found," 76. See also McCormack, "Grace and Being: The Role of God's Gracious Election in Karl Barth's Theological Ontology," in *The Cambridge Companion to Karl Barth*, ed. John Webster (Cambridge: Cambridge University Press, 2002), 92–110; Paul Molnar, "Can the Electing God be God Without Us? Some Implications of

Bruce McCormack's Understanding of Barth's Doctrine of Election for the Doctrine of the Trinity," *Neue Zeitschrift für Systematische Theologie und Religionsphilosophie*, 49.2 (2002): 199–222, and Molnar, *Divine Freedom and the Doctrine of the Immanent Trinity: In Dialogue with Karl Barth and Contemporary Theology* (Edinburgh: T&T Clark, 2002). Although I find McCormack's interpretation compelling and hope to take it up in future work, it is not necessary to argue that the incarnation is constitutive of the triunity of God in order to develop a two-*ousiai* creation Christology, so I will forego further engagement here.

34 Barth, *Church Dogmatics*, vol. 3, *The Doctrine of Creation*, part 1, ed. G. W. Bromiley and T. F. Torrance (Peabody, Mass: Hendrickson, 2010), §1, 3. Subsequent references are to this edition.

35 This election is an outpouring of divine love; as Barth argues, "God in His love elects another to fellowship with Himself. . . . He constitutes Himself as benefit or favour, and in so doing He elects another as an object of his love." Barth, *CD* II.2, 10; see also *CD* II.2, 43.

36 Barth, *Church Dogmatics*, vol. 3, *The Doctrine of Creation*, part 4, ed. G. W. Bromiley and T. F. Torrance (Peabody, Mass: Hendrickson, 2010), §2, 39–40. Subsequent references are to this edition.

37 Barth, *CD* II.2, 54.

38 Although approaching the question from a different angle, Karl Rahner articulates something similar when he says, "God does not merely create something other than himself—he also gives himself to this other. . . . The end is the absolute beginning. This beginning is not the infinite emptiness or nothingness, but the fullness which alone explains the divided and that which begins, which alone can support a becoming and which alone can give to that which begins the real power of movement towards something more developed and at the same time more intimate." Rahner, "Christology within an Evolutionary View," in Rahner, *Theological Investigations*, vol. 5, *Later Writings*, trans. Karl H. Kruger (1966; New York: Seabury, 1975), 171–72.

39 Barth, *CD* II.2, 8 (emphasis added).

40 Barth, *CD* II.2, 43.

41 Barth, *CD* II.2, 7.

42 According to Barth, "As the subject and object of this choice, Jesus Christ was at the beginning. . . . He was at the beginning of all things, at the beginning of God's dealing with the reality which is distinct from Himself. Jesus Christ was the choice or election of God in respect of this reality." *CD* II.2, 102. See also *CD* III.1, 42: "The purpose and therefore the meaning of creation is to make possible the history of God's covenant with man which has its beginning, its centre, and its culmination in Jesus Christ."

43 See Barth, *CD* II.2, 53 (emphasis added):

In this name we may now discern the divine decision as an event in human history *and therefore as the substance of all the preceding history of Israel and the hope of all the succeeding history of the Church.* What happened was this, that under this name God Himself became man, that He became this particular man, and *as such the Representative of the whole people that hastens towards this man and derives from Him.* What happened was this, that under this name God Himself realized in time, and therefore as an object of human perception, the self-giving of Himself as the Covenant-partner of the people *determined by Him from and to all eternity.*

44 Barth claims, "He created the universe in Jesus Christ. That is, Jesus Christ was the meaning and purpose of His creation of the universe." *CD* III.4, 40.
45 McCormack argues that for Barth there is no "indeterminate (or 'absolute') Logos *asarkos*," no Logos undetermined by the incarnation that logically or temporally preceded the Logos *incarnandus*, "the Logos 'to be incarnate.'" McCormack, "Grace and Being: The Role of God's Gracious Election in Karl Barth's Theological Ontology," in *The Cambridge Companion to Karl Barth*, ed John Webster (Cambridge: Cambridge University Press, 2002), 94.
46 As Gregersen explains, "When the world is said to be created 'out of nothing,' it is because it has its only source in God's love. Being created *ex nihilo* is the cosmological correlate of being created *ex amore dei.*" Gregersen, "Deep Incarnation and *Kenosis*, 258.
47 Irenaeus argues that only through the incarnation could human beings have learned what was necessary: "For in no other way could we have learned the things of God, unless our Master, existing as the Word, had become man. For no other being had the power of revealing to us the things of the Father, except His own proper Word.... Again, we could have learned in no other way than by seeing our Teacher, and hearing His voice with our own ears, that, having become imitators of His works as well as doers of His words, we may have communion with Him," *Against Heresies* 5.1.1. Furthermore, Irenaeus argued that the incarnation was necessary for the fulfillment of human destiny, which includes our ultimate glorification: "For it was for this end that the Word of God was made man, and He who was the Son of God became the Son of man, that man, having been taken into the Word, and receiving the adoption, might become the son of God." *Against Heresies* 3.19.1.
48 Holmes Rolston III raises this argument, pointing out that "real effects all the way back in time would require reverse causation, which is not permitted in contemporary physics." Rolston, "Divine Presence," 262.
49 This also highlights the challenge of how the incarnation could affect those who lived and died prior to birth of Jesus, discussed above.
50 Brian Leftow, "A Timeless God Incarnate," in *The Incarnation*, ed. Davis, Kendall, and O'Collins, 273–74.

51 See Oliver Crisp's description of this traditional view:

> If God is timeless, then there is a sense in which the Word is eternally God Incarnate. There is no time at which he becomes Incarnate on this view, because time has not application to an a-temporal being. So it is not the case, on this timelessness view of God that before the Incarnation the Word was non-Incarnate, but from the Incarnation onward became incarnate. Rather, if the Word is timeless, he is timelessly God Incarnate, although the human Jesus of Nazareth begins to exist at a certain time.

Crisp, *God Incarnate: Explorations in Christology* (New York: T&T Clark, 2009), 58.

52 See Barth's claim:

> The answer given by the life of Jesus to the questions of God and man makes His time the time which always was when men lived, which always is when they live, and which always will be when they will live. It makes this life at once the centre and the beginning and end of all the times.... It is the time of man in its whole extent. Wherever men live and have time the decision taken in the life of Jesus holds good: the content of His life affects and embraces them all because it is the answer to the question which God addresses to all men and which they address to God.

CD III.2, 440. Restated in terms of two *ousiai*, this would mean that the time of Jesus is the time when creation existed, which always is when it exists, and which always will be when it exists. George Hunsinger argues that "what needs to happen—and in Christ's resurrection and ascension what does happen—is for this reconciliation to be made contemporaneous with the rest of history. Easter involves Christ's 'transition to a presence which is eternal and therefore embraces all times.'" *CD* IV.1, 318. Hunsinger, "Karl Barth's Christology," 138.

53 This appeals to the same logic as McCormack's reading of the Logos *incarnandus* in Barth; see n. 43 above. Leftow illustrates this claim by way of analogy to a brick wall, arguing that,

> The Son is the first part of this whole [Son, soul, and body] to exist. But the first part of a whole *is* part of that whole. The first brick laid in a certain place is the beginning of a wall.... The brick is the first part of the wall as soon as it is laid. It does not wait to become so until there are enough bricks to count as a wall of which it is part.... The Son is part of a human composite as soon as the Son exists, even if the rest of the composite does not yet exist—for the rest of the composite *is* surely coming.

Leftow, "A Timeless God Incarnate," 296–97.

54 The first view is generally connected to Plato's understanding of the Forms or Ideals, the second more frequently associated with Aristotle and the categories, while the final is a more recent development. Without mounting an involved argument as to the superiority of any one approach outlined here, I will demonstrate how created *ousia* functions in each metaphysical system and what the preliminary definition of created *ousia* developed in chapter 2 suggests about the complex interdependence of these alternatives.

55 Paul D. Janz, "Metaphysics," in *Cambridge Dictionary of Christian Theology*, ed. McFarlan, Fergusson, Kilby, and Torrance, 309. For a discussion of how this relates to the question at hand, see Edwin van Driel's discussion of whether Barth's Christology holds that the Word assumes a particular human being (what van Driel refers to as primary substance) or humanity in general (which van Driel calls secondary substance). Arguing that Barth is imprecise in his distinctions between the two substances, van Driel proposes that the Word could fulfill the purpose of the incarnation—enabling divine friendship with creatures—only by assuming one particular person. Van Driel, *Incarnation Anyway*, 163–66.

56 Wesley Wildman defines relational ontology, observing, "the basic contention of relational ontology is simply that the relations between entities are ontologically more fundamental than the entities themselves. This contrasts with substantivist ontology in which entities are ontologically primary and relations ontologically derivative." Wesley J. Wildman, "An Introduction to Relational Ontology," in *The Trinity and an Entangled World: Relationality in Physical Science and Theology*, ed. John C. Polkinghorne (Grand Rapids: Eerdmans, 2010), 55. In a nuanced historical examination of Christian ontological assumptions, Sarah Coakley challenges the notion that relational ontology is either new or necessarily in a mutually exclusive relationship to substantive ontology. See Sarah Coakley, "Afterword: 'Relational Ontology,' Trinity, and Science," in *The Trinity and an Entangled World*, ed. Polkinghorne, 184–99.

57 Although some theists might be tempted to postulate God, prior to the creation of the universe, as such a solitary entity, such a thought-experiment would fail on two grounds. The first is that the Creator was already in relationship to that which would be created in much the same way that the Logos is always *incarnandus*. The second is that for Christians, the doctrine of the Trinity precludes consideration of God as a single solitary entity with no differentiation.

58 This argument resonates with Coakley's "skepticism that a choice between Trinitarian 'hypostatization' and 'relationality' (in terms of ontological priority) is either desirable theologically, or indeed mandated by our authoritative Patristic sources." Coakley, "Afterword," 194.

59 One traditional response to this charge is that existence itself is a gift, and we can therefore have no claims of justice on God. That is, if God chooses to create some creatures and not save (or even condemn) them, that is no violation of

justice. Although there is legal merit to such an argument, it does not respond to the ethical impulse behind these objections, nor does it agree with biblical portraits of God as merciful, loving, or kind.

5 CREATED TOGETHER

1. N. Tanner, *Decrees of the Ecumenical Councils*, 51.
2. Philippians 2:6-8 describes Jesus as one, "who, though he was in the form of God, did not regard equality with God as something to be exploited, but emptied himself, taking the form of a slave, being born in human likeness. And being found in human form, he humbled himself and became obedient to the point of death—even death on a cross."
3. David P. Moessner, "Turning Status 'Upside Down' in Philippi: Christ Jesus' 'Emptying Himself' as Forfeiting Any Acknowledgement of His 'Equality with God' (Phil 2:6-11)," *Horizons in Biblical Theology* 31 (2009): 123–143. See also Michael W. Martin and Bryan A. Nash, "Philippians 2:6–11 As Subversive Hymnos: A Study in the Light of Ancient Rhetorical Theory," *The Journal of Theological Studies* 66.1 (2015): 90–138.
4. For example, see Aquinas' argument that human nature is fit for the incarnation "according to its dignity, because human nature, as being rational and intellectual, was made for attaining to the Word to some extent by its operation, by knowing and loving Him ... in the irrational creature the fitness of dignity is wanting." Aquinas, *ST* 3.4.1. For a discussion of human fitness according to need, see below.
5. In addition to his argument that human nature is "fit" for the incarnation by its dignity, Aquinas also argues that it is fit "according to its need—because it stood in need of restoration, having fallen under original sin." Aquinas, *ST* 3.4.1.
6. Athanasius make a very similar argument, noting that,

   > Men, having rejected the contemplation of God, and ... feigning gods for themselves of mortal men and demons; to this end the loving and general Saviour of all, the Word of God, takes to himself a body, and as man walks among men and meets the senses of all men halfway, to the end, I say, that they who think that God is corporeal may from what the Lord effects by his body perceive the truth, and through him recognize the Father. So, men as they were, and humans in all their thoughts, on whatever objects they fixed their senses, there they saw themselves met halfway.

   Athanasius, *On the Incarnation*, 69.
7. Unfortunately, in too many instances today human beings continue to deny our interdependence and remain at odds with the nature of material existence, despite the humanity of the incarnation. It is possible, however, that the situation would have been worse without the pattern of Jesus' human life.

8. Tertullian, "On the Flesh of Christ," in *The Christological Controversy*, ed. Norris, 68.
9. Johnson, *She Who Is*, 151–52.
10. Friedrich Schleiermacher, *The Christian Faith*, ed. H. R. Mackintosh and J. S. Stewart (London: T&T Clark, 1999), 16.
11. As we have previously seen, Athanasius argued that humanity was originally given the additional gift of incorruption and immortality. Athanasius, *On the Incarnation*, 58.
12. For example, mining extracts oil, coal, and natural gas at a rate that far exceeds the eons they took to accumulate, while the fishing industry cannibalizes itself by practices that lead to fishery collapses.
13. In his work on reconciliation Barth described sin as pride, sloth, and falsehood, see *CD* IV.1, 60; IV.2, 65; IV.3.1, 70. More recently, theologies that take into account the different positions of oppressors and those who are oppressed have suggested that even more nuance is necessary in contemporary accounts of sin.
14. Andrew Sung Park, *Triune Atonement: Christ's Healing for Sinners, Victims, and the Whole Creation* (Louisville: Westminster John Knox, 2009), 39.
15. Park, *Triune Atonement*, 39–45.
16. Park, *Triune Atonement*, 74–90.
17. "Sin or injustice causes *han*, and *han* produces sin or injustice.... Unattended or unhealed *han* gives rise to evil. This evil can regenerate hand and sin. Also, sin and *han* collaborate to engender evil. They overlap in many tragic areas of life." Park, *Triune Atonement*, 41.
18. Darby Kathleen Ray, *Deceiving the Devil: Atonement, Abuse, and Ransom* (Cleveland: Pilgrim, 1998), 31.
19. Ray, *Deceiving the Devil*, 31–32.
20. McCormack, "Seek God Where He May Be Found," 67.
21. Van Driel, "Karl Barth on the Eternal Existence of Jesus Christ," 54.
22. McFague, *The Body of God*, 49–50.
23. Willis Jenkins argues that "ethics can begin from that incompetence ... when reform projects take their incompetence as a demand to create new possibilities from their inherited traditions." Jenkins, *The Future of Ethics: Sustainability, Social Justice, and Religious Creativity* (Washington, D.C.: Georgetown University Press, 2013), 6.

BIBLIOGRAPHY

Abrams, Marc D. "Effects of Burning Regime on Buried Seed Banks and Canopy Coverage in a Kansas Tallgrass Prairie." *The Southwestern Naturalist* 33.1 (1988): 65–70.

Alexander of Alexandria. *Letter to Alexander of Thessalonica.* In *The Trinitarian Controversy*, edited by William G. Rusch, 33–44. Philadelphia: Fortress, 1980.

Andrews, Candice Gaukel. "The Trees Are Talking." *Good Nature Travel.* September 20, 2011. http://goodnature.nathab.com/the-trees-are-talking/.

Anselm of Canterbury. *Cur Deus Homo.* In *Basic Writings*, edited and translated by Thomas Williams. Indianapolis: Hackett, 2007.

———. *Proslogium.* In *St. Anselm: Proslogium; Monologium; An Appendix in Behalf of the Fool by Gaunilon; and Cur Deus Homo*, edited and translated by Sidney Norton Deane. Eugene, Ore.: Wipf & Stock, 2003.

Apollinaris of Laodicea. *Fragments.* In *The Christological Controversy*, edited by Richard A. Norris, 107–11. Philadelphia: Fortress, 1980.

Aquinas, Thomas. *Summa Theologica.* Christian Classics Ethereal Library, n.d. https://www.ccel.org/ccel/aquinas/summa.

Aristotle. *On the Soul.* In *The Basic Works of Aristotle*, edited by Richard McKeon, 535-603. New York: Random House, 1941.

Arius. *Letter to Alexander of Alexandria.* In *The Trinitarian Controversy*, edited by William G. Rusch, 31–32. Philadelphia: Fortress, 1980.

———. *Letter to Eusebius of Nicomedia.* In *The Trinitarian Controversy*, edited by William G. Rusch, 29–30. Philadelphia: Fortress, 1980.

Athanasius. *On the Incarnation of the Word.* In *Christology of the Later Fathers*, edited by Edward R. Hardy, 55–110. Philadelphia: Westminster, 1954. Repr., Louisville: Westminster John Knox, 2006.

"AT&T TV Commercial—It's Not Complicated 'Grandma.'" YouTube video, 0:30. Posted by "H. Jay Yun" on January 3, 2013. https://www.youtube.com/watch?v=fG3_kC5GxvO.

Aulén, Gustaf. *Christus Victor: An Historical Study of the Three Main Types of the Idea of Atonement*. 1931; Eugene, Ore.: Wipf & Stock, 2003.

Badham, Linda, and Paul Badham. *Immortality or Extinction?* London: Macmillan, 1982.

Barbour, Ian G. *Religion and Science: Historical and Contemporary Issues*. San Francisco: HarperCollins, 1997.

Barth, Karl. *Church Dogmatics*. Edited by G. W. Bromiley and T. F. Torrance. Peabody, Mass.: Hendrickson, 1995.

———. *Epistle to the Romans*. Translated by Edwyn C. Hoskyns. Oxford: Oxford University Press, 1968.

Bauckham, Richard. "The Incarnation and the Cosmic Christ." In *Incarnation: On the Scope and Depth of Christology*, edited by Niels Henrik Gregersen, 25–57. Minneapolis: Fortress, 2015.

Beisner, E. Calvin. *Where Garden Meets Wilderness*. Grand Rapids: Eerdmans, 1997.

Braine, David. "Cosmological Arguments." In *Philosophy of Religion: A Guide to the Subject*, edited by Brian Davies, 42–58. Washington D.C.: Georgetown University Press, 1998.

Bunnin, Nicholas, and Jiyuan Yu, eds. "Genus" and "Infima Species." In *The Blackwell Dictionary of Western Philosophy*, 282 and 345. Malden: Blackwell Publishers, 2004.

Carter, J. Kameron. *Race: A Theological Account*. Oxford: Oxford University Press, 2008.

Clarke, W. Norris. "A New Look at the Immutability of God." In *God: Knowable and Unknowable*, edited by Robert J. Roth. New York: Fordham University Press, 1973.

Clayton, Nicola S., and Anthony Dickinson. "Episodic-like Memory during Cache Recovery by Scrub Jays." *Nature* 395.6699 (1998): 272.

Coakley, Sarah. "Afterword: 'Relational Ontology,' Trinity, and Science." In *The Trinity and an Entangled World: Relationality in Physical Science and Theology*, edited by John C. Polkinghorne, 184–99. Grand Rapids: Eerdmans, 2010.

———. *God, Sexuality, and the Self: An Essay 'On the Trinity.'* Cambridge: Cambridge University Press, 2013.

———. "What Does Chalcedon Solve and What Does It Not? Some Reflections on the Status and Meaning of the Chalcedonian 'Definition.'" In *The Incarnation: An Interdisciplinary Symposium on the Incarnation of the Son of God*, edited by Stephen T. Davis, Daniel Kendall, SJ, and Gerald O'Collins, SJ, 143–63. Oxford: Oxford University Press, 2002.

Cobb Jr., John B. Foreword to *Fidelity with Plausibility: Modest Christologies in the Twentieth Century*, by Wesley J. Wildman. Albany: State University of New York, 1998.

Cobb Jr., John B., and David Ray Griffin. *Process Theology: An Introductory Exposition*. Louisville: Westminster John Knox, 1976.

Cone, James. *God of the Oppressed*. New York: Seabury, 1975.

Copeland, Rebecca. "Ecomimetic Interpretation: Ascertainment, Identification, and Dialogue in Matthew 6:24–34." *Biblical Interpretation*, forthcoming.

———. "It's Not Complicated." *Placing American Religions*, March 21, 2013. https://scholarblogs.emory.edu/placingamericanreligions/author/rlcopel/.

Crisp, Oliver. *God Incarnate: Explorations in Christology*. New York: T&T Clark, 2009.

Cyril of Alexandria. *Against Nestorius*. In *Cyril of Alexandria*, edited by Norman Russell, 130–74. London: Routledge, 2000.

———. *An Explanation of The Twelve Chapters*. In *Cyril of Alexandria*, edited by Norman Russell, 175–89. London: Routledge, 2000.

Daley, Brian E., SJ. "Divine Transcendence and Human Transformation: Gregory of Nyssa's Anti-Apollinarian Christology." In *Re-Thinking Gregory of Nyssa*, edited by Sarah Coakley, 67–76. Malden: Blackwell, 2003.

Dally, Joanna M., Nathan J. Emery, and Nicola S. Clayton. "Avian Theory of Mind and Counter Espionage by Food-Caching Western Scrub-Jays (Aphelocoma Californica)." *European Journal of Developmental* 7.1 (2010): 17–37.

Daly, Mary. *Beyond God the Father: Toward a Philosophy of Women's Liberation*. Boston: Beacon, 1973.

Darwin, Charles. *On the Origin of Species*. London: John Murray, 1859.

Davis, Stephen T. *Logic and the Nature of God*. Grand Rapids: Eerdmans, 1983.

Dennett, Daniel C. *Darwin's Dangerous Idea: Evolution and the Meanings of Life*. New York: Penguin Books, 1995.

De Waal, Frans. *Are We Smart Enough to Know How Smart Animals Are?* New York: Norton, 2016.

Dionysius the Areopagite. *On the Divine Names and The Mystical Theology*. Translated by C. E. Rolt. New York: Macmillan, 1957.

Douglas, Kelly Brown. *The Black Christ*. Maryknoll, N.Y.: Orbis Books, 1994.

Edwards, Denis. "Incarnation and the Natural World: Explorations in the Tradition of Athanasius." In *Incarnation: On the Scope and Depth of Christology*, edited by Niels Henrik Gregersen, 157–76. Minneapolis: Fortress, 2015

Englesiepen, Jane. "Trees Communicate: 'Mother Trees' Use Fungal Communication Systems to Preserve Forests." *Ecology*. October 8, 2012. http://www.ecology.com/2012/10/08/trees-communicate/.

Eusebius of Caesarea. *Letter to His Church*. In *The Trinitarian Controversy*, edited by William G. Rusch, 57–60. Philadelphia: Fortress, 1980.

Fleming, Nic. "Plants Talk to Each Other Using an Internet of Fungus." BBC. November 11, 2014. http://www.bbc.com/earth/story/20141111-plants-have-a-hidden-internet.

Fox, Matthew. *The Coming of the Cosmic Christ: The Healing of Mother Earth and the Birth of a Global Renaissance.* San Francisco: Harper & Row, 1988.

Geach, P. T. *Logic Matters.* Oxford: Blackwell, 1972.

Gregersen, Niels Henrik. "The Cross of Christ in an Evolutionary World." *Dialog* 40.3 (2001): 192–207.

———. "Deep Incarnation and *Kenosis*: In, With, and As: A Response to Ted Peters." *Dialog* 52.3 (2013), 251–62.

———. "The Extended Body of Christ." In *Incarnation: On the Scope and Depth of Christology*, edited by Niels Henrik Gregersen, 225–51. Minneapolis: Fortress Press, 2015.

Gregory of Nazianzus. *Letter 101: The First Letter to Cledonius the Presbyter.* In *On God and Christ: The Five Theological Orations and Two Letters to Cledonius*, translated by Lionel Wickham and Frederick Williams, 155–66. Crestwood, N.Y.: St. Vladimir's Seminary Press, 2002.

Gregory of Nyssa. *Address on Religious Instruction.* In *Christology of the Later Fathers*, edited by Edward R. Hardy, 268–25. Philadelphia: Westminster, 1954. Repr., Louisville: Westminster John Knox, 2006.

Guroian, Vigen. "Salvation as Divine Therapy." *Theology Today* 61 (2004): 309–21.

Habel, Norman C. "Introducing the Earth Bible." In *Readings from the Perspective of Earth*, edited by Norman C. Habel, 25–37. Sheffield: Sheffield Academic Press, 2000.

Hall, Matthew. *Plants as Persons: A Philosophical Botany.* Albany: SUNY Press, 2011.

Hartshorne, Charles. *Omnipotence and Other Theological Mistakes.* Albany: State University of New York Press, 1984.

Hick, John. "Jesus and the World Religions." In *The Myth of God Incarnate*, edited by John Hick, 167–85. Philadelphia: Westminster, 1977.

———. *The Metaphor of God Incarnate: Christology in a Pluralistic Age.* Louisville: Westminster John Knox, 1993.

Hunsinger, George. "Karl Barth's Christology: Its Basic Chalcedonian Character." In *The Cambridge Companion to Karl Barth*, edited by John Webster, 127–42. Cambridge: Cambridge University Press, 2002.

Irenaeus. *Against Heresies.* In vol. 1 of *The Ante-Nicene Fathers.* Edited by Alexander Roberts and James Donaldson. Grand Rapids: Christian Classics Ethereal Library. https://www.ccel.org/ccel/schaff/anf01.ix.iv.xix.html.

Janz, Paul D. "Metaphysics." In *The Cambridge Dictionary of Christian Theology*, edited by Ian A. McFarland, David A. S. Furgusson, Karen Kilby, and Ian R. Torrence, 309. Cambridge: Cambridge University Press, 2011.

Jenkins, Willis. *The Future of Ethics: Sustainability, Social Justice, and Religious Creativity.* Washington, D.C.: Georgetown University Press, 2013.

Johnson, Elizabeth A. *Ask the Beasts: Darwin and the Love of God.* London: Bloomsbury, 2014.

———. *Creation and the Cross: The Mercy of God for a Planet in Peril.* Maryknoll, N.Y.: Orbis Books, 2018.

———. "Jesus and the Cosmos: Soundings in Deep Incarnation." In *Incarnation: On the Scope and Depth of Christology*, edited by Niels Henrik Gregersen, 133–56. Minneapolis: Fortress, 2015.

———. *She Who Is: The Mystery of God in Feminist Theological Discourse.* New York: Crossroad, 1992.

Kainz, Howard P. *The Philosophy of Human Nature.* Chicago: Open Court, 2008.

Kierkegaard, Søren. *Training in Christianity.* Translated by Walter Lowrie. Oxford: Oxford Univeristy Press, 1941.

King, Hobart M. "Limestone: What Is Limestone and How Is It Used?" http://geology.com/rocks/limestone.shtml.

King, Peter. "Scotus on Metaphysics." In *The Cambridge Companion to Duns Scotus*, edited by Thomas Williams, 15–68. Cambridge: Cambridge University Press, 2006.

Kretzman, Norman. "Omniscience and Immutability." In *Philosophy of Religion*, edited by William Rowe and William Wainwright, 60–70. New York: Harcourt, Brace, Jovanovich, 1973.

LaCugna, Catherine Mowry. *God For Us: The Trinity and Christian Life.* New York: HarperSanFrancisco, 1993.

"Leaf Cutter Ants." Oakland Zoo Conservation & Education. http://www.oaklandzoo.org/leaf-cutter-ant.

Leftow, Brian. "A Timeless God Incarnate." In *The Incarnation: An Interdisciplinary Symposium on the Incarnation of the Son of God*, edited by Stephen T. Davis, Daniel Kendall, SJ, and Gerald O'Collins, SJ. Oxford: Oxford University Press, 2002.

Linzy, Andrew. *Animal Theology.* Urbana: University of Illinois Press, 1994.

Lovelock, James. "Gaia: The Living Earth." *Nature* 426.6968 (2003): 769–70.

Lyons, J. A. *The Cosmic Christ in Origen and Teilhard de Chardin.* Oxford: Oxford University Press, 1982.

MacIntyre, Alasdair C. *After Virtue: A Study in Moral Theory.* 3rd ed. Notre Dame: University of Notre Dame Press, 2007.

Mann, William E. "Duns Scotus on Natural and Supernatural Knowledge of God." In *The Cambridge Companion to Duns Scotus*, edited by Thomas Williams, 238–62. Cambridge: Cambridge University Press, 2006.

Martin, Michael W., and Bryan A. Nash. "Philippians 2:6-11 As Subversive Hymnos: A Study in the Light of Ancient Rhetorical Theory." *The Journal of Theological Studies* 66.1 (2015): 90–138.

Maximus the Confessor. *Difficulty 41.* In *Maximus the Confessor*, edited by Andrew Louth, 155–62. London: Routledge, 1996.

Mayr, Ernst. *Systematics and the Origin of Species.* New York: Dover, 1964.

McCormack, Bruce. "Grace and Being: The Role of God's Gracious Election in Karl Barth's Theological Ontology." In *The Cambridge Companion to Karl*

Barth*, edited by John Webster, 92–110. Cambridge: Cambridge University Press, 2002.

———. "Seek God Where He May Be Found: A Response to Edwin Christian van Driel." *Scottish Journal of Theology* 60.1 (2007): 62–79.

McFague, Sallie. *The Body of God: An Ecological Theology*. Minneapolis: Augsburg Fortess, 1993.

McFarland, Ian A. *Difference and Identity: A Theological Anthropology*. Cleveland: Pilgrim Press, 2001.

———. "Theological Anthropology." In *The Cambridge Dictionary of Christian of Theology*, edited by Ian A. McFarland, David A. S. Furgusson, Karen Kilby, and Iain R. Torrance, 501–4. Cambridge: Cambridge University Press, 2011.

McLaughlin, Ryan Patrick. *Preservation and Protest: Theological Foundations for an Eco-Eschatalogical Ethics*. Minneapolis: Fortress, 2014.

"Megyn Kelly: 'Santa Is What He Is,' Which Is White." YouTube video, 2:10. Posted by "TMP TV" on December 12, 2013. https://www.youtube.com/watch?v=7XYlJqf4dLI.

Meyer, Sebastian T. "Ecosystem Engineering by Leaf-Cutting Ants: Nests of Atta Cephalotes Drastically Alter Forest Structure and Microclimate." *Ecological Entomology* 36.1 (2011): 14–24.

Moessner, David P. "Turning Status 'Upside Down' in Philippi: Christ Jesus' 'Emptying Himself' as Forfeiting Any Acknowledgement of His 'Equality with God' (Phil 2:6-11)." *Horizons in Biblical Theology* 31 (2009): 123–43.

Molnar, Paul. "Can the Electing God Be God without Us? Some Implications of Bruce McCormack's Understanding of Barth's Doctrine of Election for the Doctrine of the Trinity." *Neue Zeitschrift für Systematische Theologie und Religionsphilosophie*, 49.2 (2002): 199–222.

———. *Divine Freedom and the Doctrine of the Immanent Trinity: In Dialogue with Karl Barth and Contemporary Theology*. Edinburgh: T&T Clark, 2002.

Moltmann, Jürgen. *The Coming of God: Christian Eschatology*. Translated by Margaret Kohl. Minneapolis: Fortress, 1996.

———. "Is God Incarnate in All That Is?" In *Incarnation: On the Scope and Depth of Christology*, edited by Niels Henrik Gregersen, 119–31. Minneapolis: Fortress, 2015.

———. *The Way of Jesus Christ: Christology in Messianic Dimensions* (San Francisco: HarperSanFrancisco, 1990).

Morris, Thomas V. *The Logic of God Incarnate*. Eugene, Ore.: Wipf & Stock, 1986.

Palmer, Brian, and Seth Freed Wessler. "The Costs of the Confederacy." *Smithsonian Magazine*, December 2018. https://www.smithsonianmag.com/history/costs-confederacy-special-report-180970731/.

"Pando, the Trembling Giant." *Atlas Obscura*. http://www.atlasobscura.com/places/pando-the-trembling-giant.

Park, Andrew Sung. *Triune Atonement: Christ's Healing for Sinners, Victims, and the Whole Creation*. Louisville: Westminster John Knox, 2009.

Pawl, Timothy. *In Defense of Conciliar Christology: A Philosophical Essay*. Oxford: Oxford University Press, 2016.

Pelikan, Jaroslav. *Jesus Christ Through the Centuries: His Place in the History of Culture*. New Haven: Yale University Press, 1985.

Perler, Dominik. "Duns Scotus's Philosophy of Language." In *The Cambridge Companion to Duns Scotus*, edited by Thomas Williams, 161–92. Cambridge: Cambridge University Press, 2006.

Peters, Ted. "Happy Danes and Deep Incarnation." *Dialog* 52.3 (2013): 244–50.

Polkinghorne, John. "Afterword: Reservations." In *Incarnation: On the Scope and Depth of Christology*, edited by Niels Henrik Gregersen, 355-359. Minneapolis: Fortress, 2015.

Pope Paul VI. "Decree on Apostolate of the Laity." November 18, 1965. http://www.vatican.va/archive/hist_councils/ii_vatican_council/documents/vat-ii_decree_19651118_apostolicam-actuositatem_en.html.

Rahner, Karl. *Theological Investigations*, volume 5: *Later Writings*. Translated by Karl H. Kruger. 1966; New York: Seabury, 1975. 157–92.

Rasmussen, Larry. *Earth-Honoring Faith: Religious Ethics in a New Key*. Oxford: Oxford University Press, 2013.

Ray, Darby Kathleen. *Deceiving the Devil: Atonement, Abuse, and Ransom*. Cleveland: Pilgrim, 1998.

Reichman, O. J. *Konza Prairie: A Tallgrass Natural History*. Lawrence: University Press of Kansas, 1987.

Reis, Bárbara Monique dos Santos, Aline Silva, Martín Roberto Alvarez, Tássio Brito de Oliveira, and Andre Rodrigues. "Fungal Communities in Gardens of the Leafcutter Ant Atta Cephalotes in Forest and Cabruca Agrosystems of Southern Bahia State (Brazil)." *Fungal Biology* 119.12 (2015): 1170–78.

"Resolution on Global Warming." Southern Baptist Convention. 2007. http://www.sbc.net/resolutions/1171/on-global-warming.

Rhoades, David F. "Responses of Alder and Willow to Attack by Tent Caterpillars and Webworms: Evidence for Pheromonal Sensitivity of Willows." In *Plant Resistance to Insects*, edited by Paul A. Hedin, 55–68. Washington, D.C.: American Chemical Society, 1983.

Ridley, Mark. *The Problems of Evolution*. New York: Oxford University Press, 1985.

Rolston III, Holmes. "Divine Presence: Causal, Cybernetic, Caring, Cruciform." In *Incarnation: On the Scope and Depth of Christology*, edited by Niels Henrik Gregersen, 255–87. Minneapolis: Fortress, 2015.

———. "Does Nature Need to Be Redeemed?" *Zygon* 29 (1994): 205–29.

Ruether, Rosemary Radford. "The Liberation of Christology from Patriarchy." *Religion and Intellectual Life* 2.3 (1985): 116–28.

———. *Sexism and God-Talk: Toward a Feminist Theology*. Boston: Beacon, 1983.

Russell, Robert John. "Jesus: The Way of All Flesh and the Proleptic Feather of Time." In *Incarnation: On the Scope and Depth of Christology*, edited by Neils Henrik Gregersen, 331–49. Minneapolis: Fortress, 2015.

Sallman, Warner. *Head of Christ*, 1940. The Warner Sallman Collection. http://www.warnersallman.com/collection/images/head-of-christ/.

"Sankofa." University of Illinois Springfield. https://www.uis.edu/africanamericanstudies/students/sankofa/.

Santmire, H. Paul. "Toward a Cosmic Christology: A Kerygmatic Proposal." *Theology and Science* 9.3 (2011): 287–305.

Santmire, H. Paul, and John B. Cobb Jr. "The World of Nature According to the Protestant Tradition." In *The Oxford Handbook of Religion and Ecology*, edited by Roger S. Gottlieb, 115–46. Oxford: Oxford University Press, 2010.

Schleiermacher, Friedrich. *The Christian Faith*. Edited by H. R. Mackintosh and J. S. Stewart. London: T&T Clark, 1999.

Scott, Jimmy. "Aphelocoma Californica: Western Scrub Jay." University of Michigan Animal Diversity Web. http://animaldiversity.org/accounts/Aphelocoma_californica/.

Sender, Ron, Shai Fuchs, and Ron Milo. "Revised Estimates for the Number of Human and Bacteria Cells in the Body." *PLoS Biology* 14.8 (2016): 1–14.

Seper, Franjo Cardinal. "Declaration on the Question of Admission of Women to the Ministerial Priesthood." October 15, 1976. http://www.vatican.va/roman_curia/congregations/cfaith/documents/rc_con_cfaith_doc_19761015_inter-insigniores_en.html.

Shadmon, Asher. *Stone in Israel*. Jerusalem: State of Israel Ministry of Development Natural Resource Research Organization, 1972.

Sittler, Joseph. "Called to Unity." In *Evocations of Grace: Writings on Ecology, Theology, and Ethics*, edited by Steven Bouma-Prediger and Peter Bakken, 38–50. Grand Rapids: Eerdmans, 2000.

Smithsonian Institution. "Numbers of Insects (Species and Individuals)." National Museum of Natural History, Entomology Section, Department of Systematic Biology, Information Sheet 18, https://www.si.edu/encyclopedia_si/nmnh/buginfo/bugnos.htm.

Soulen, Kendall. *The God of Israel and Christian Theology*. Minneapolis: Fortress, 1996.

Southgate, Christopher. "Depth, Sign and Destiny." In *Incarnation: On the Scope and Depth of Christology*, edited by Niels Henrik Gregersen, 203–23. Minneapolis: Fortress, 2015.

———. "Does God's Care Make Any Difference? Theological Reflection on the Suffering of God's Creatures." In *Christian Faith and the Earth: Current Paths and Emerging Horizons in Ecotheology*, edited by Ernst M. Conradie, Sigured Bergmann, Celia Deane-Drummond, and Denis Edwards, 97–114. London: Bloomsbury, 2014.

———. *The Groaning of Creation: God, Evolution and the Problem of Evil.* Louisville: Westminster John Knox, 2008.

Stead, Christopher. *Divine Substance.* Oxford: Oxford University Press, 1977.

Steenberg, M. C. *Irenaeus on Creation: The Cosmic Christ and the Saga of Redemption.* Boston: Brill, 2008.

Studtmann, Paul. "Aristotle's Categories." In *The Stanford Encyclopedia of Philosophy*, edited by Edward N. Zalta. Stanford University, Summer 2014. http://plato.stanford.edu/archives/sum2014/entries/aristotle-categories/.

Suen, Garret, et al. "The Genome Sequence of the Leaf-Cutter Ant Atta Cephalotes Reveals Insights into Its Obligate Symbiotic Lifestyle." *Plos Genetics* 7.2 (2011): 1–11.

The Synodal Letter of the Council of Antioch, A.D. 325. In *The Trinitarian Controversy*, edited by William G. Rusch, 37–40. Philadelphia: Fortress, 1980.

Tanner, Kathryn. "Creation Ex Nihilo as Mixed Metaphor." *Modern Theology* 29.2 (2013), 138–55.

———. *Jesus, Humanity and the Trinity: A Brief Systematic Theology.* Minneapolis: Fortress, 2001.

Tanner, Norman P., ed. *Decrees of the Ecumenical Councils.* Vol. 1, *Nicaea I–Lateran V.* London: Sheed & Ward, 1990.

Teilhard de Chardin, Pierre. *Christianity and Evolution.* New York: Harcourt, Brace, Jovanovic, 1974.

———. *Science and Christ.* New York: Harper & Row, 1968.

Tertullian. "'On the Flesh of Christ.'" In *The Christological Controversy*, edited by Richard A. Norris. Philadelphia: Fortress Press, 1980.

Teste, François P., Suzanne W. Simard, Daniel M. Durall, Robert D. Guy, Melanie D. Jones, and Amanda L. Schoonmaker. "Access to Mycorrhizal Networks and Roots of Trees: Importance for Seedling Survival and Resource Transfer." *Ecology* 90.10 (2009): 2808–22.

Thom, James M., and Nicola S. Clayton. "Re-Caching by Western Scrub-Jays (*Aphelocoma Californica*) Cannot Be Attributed to Stress." *PLOS ONE* 8.1 (2013): 1–4.

Thompson, Geoff. "'Remaining Loyal to the Earth': Humanity, God's Other Creatures and the Bible in Karl Barth." In *Ecological Hermeneutics: Biblical, Historical and Theological Perspectives*, edited by David G. Horrell, Cherryl Hunt, Christopher Southgate, and Francesca Stavrakopoulou, 181–95. New York: T&T Clark, 2010.

Tollefsen, Torstein. "Saint Maximus the Confessor on Creation and Incarnation." In *Incarnation: On the Scope and Depth of Christology*, edited by Niels Henrik Gregersen, 105–8. Minneapolis: Fortress, 2015.

Trewavas, Anthony. "Aspects of Plant Intelligence." *Annals of Botany* 92 (2003): 1–20.

Turner, Denys. *The Darkness of God: Negativity in Christian Mysticism*. Cambridge: Cambridge University Press, 1995.
Uchytil, Ronald J. "Andropogon gerardii." In U.S. Department of Agriculture, Forest Service, Rocky Mountain Research Station, Fire Sciences Laboratory, *Fire Effects Information System*, https://www.fs.fed.us/database/feis/plants/graminoid/andger/all.html.
Van der Vaart, Elske, Rineke Verbrugge, and Charlotte K. Hemelrijk. "Corvid Re-Caching without 'Theory of Mind': A Model." *PLOS ONE* 7.3 (2012): 1–8.
Van Driel, Edwin Christian. *Incarnation Anyway: Arguments for Supralapsarian Christology*. Oxford: Oxford University Press, 2008.
———. "Karl Barth on the Eternal Existence of Jesus Christ." *Scottish Journal of Theology* 60.1 (2007): 45–61.
Van Inwagen, Peter. "'Ontological Arguments.'" In *Philosophy of Religion: A Guide to the Subject*, by Brian Davies, 42–58. Washington D.C.: Georgetown University Press, 1998.
Watanabe, Arii, Uri Grodzinski, and Nicola Clayton. "Western Scrub-Jays Allocate Longer Observation Time to More Valuable Information." *Animal Cognition* 17.4 (2014): 859–67.
Webster, John. *Barth*. London: Continuum, 2000.
Wennerberg, Sarah. "Big Bluestem." *USDA/NRCS Plant Guide*, https://plants.usda.gov/plantguide/pdf/pg_ange.pdf.
"Western Scrub-Jay." National Wildlife Federation. https://www.nwf.org/Educational-Resources/Wildlife-Guide/Birds/Western-Scrub-Jay.
"Western Scrub-Jays (Aphelocoma Californica)." https://www.beautyofbirds.com/westernscrubjays.html.
White, Vernon. *Atonement and Incarnation: An Essay in Universalism and Particularity*. Cambridge: Cambridge University Press, 1991.
Wildman, Wesley J. "An Introduction to Relational Ontology." In *The Trinity and an Entangled World: Relationality in Physical Science and Theology*, edited by John C. Polkinghorne, 55–73. Grand Rapids: Eerdmans, 2010.
Wiles, Maurice. "Christianity Without Incarnation?" In *The Myth of God Incarnate*, edited by John Hick, 1–10. Philadelphia: Westminster, 1977.
Wilson, E. O. *Biophilia*. Cambridge: Harvard University Press, 1984.
Xu, Xiaofei, Zhujun Wang, and Xuewu Zhang. "The Human Microbiota Associated with Overall Health." *Critical Reviews in Biotechnology* 35.1 (2015): 129–40.
Yackulic, Charles B., and Owen T. Lewis. "Temporal Variation in Foraging Activity and Efficiency and the Role of Hitchhiking Behaviour in the Leaf-Cutting Ant, Atta Cephalotes." *Entomologia Experimentalis et Applicata* 125.2 (2007): 125–34.

INDEX

Alexander of Alexandria, 17–18, 23, 104, 107
androcentrism, 10, 24, 28–30, 33, 52, 80, 92, 99
animals, 56, 67, 79, 116, 124; bodies, 41–44, 49, 83; cognition, 44–47; soul, 34
Anselm of Canterbury, 4, 51–52, 54, 58, 63, 94–95, 103, 105, 116–17, 119
anthropomorphism, 44, 50, 78
Apollinaris of Laodicea, 20, 105, 106
apophatic theology, 50–51, 54–55, 57, 95, 116, 118
apostolic fathers, 14
Aquinas, Thomas, 21, 53–55, 59, 107, 110, 117–19, 131
Arianism, 8, 23, 60
Aristotle, 20–22, 38, 40–41, 44, 50, 100, 106–7, 109, 130
Arius of Alexandria, 17–18, 104
ascension, 72, 75, 129
Athanasius of Alexandria, 9, 15–16, 37, 47, 98–99, 102–5, 107, 112, 121–22, 131–32
Augustine, 21, 110

Barth, Karl, 63, 69–72, 92, 97–98, 105, 114, 125–29, 132

Big Bang theory, 27
Big Bluestem (*Andropogon gerardii*), 38–41, 43–44, 48, 57, 67, 112
Bonaventure, 106, 111, 124

cataphatic theology, 51, 54, 116
Catholic Church, 2
Chalcedon, Council of, 7–8, 13, 19, 22, 73, 97–98, 100, 106–7, 120–21, 125
challenges to the incarnation: coherence, 2, 3–5, 8, 11–12, 58–62, 63–64, 75, 77, 94–95; justice, 2–3, 8, 11–12, 28–31, 93, 96; plausibility, 2, 5–6, 8, 11–12, 64, 74–75, 77, 96
change processes, 37, 39, 41, 52, 56
classical theism, 54–55, 57, 59, 62, 118
Clement of Alexandria, 99
climate, 2, 36
cognition, 44–47, 66–67, 75, 115
colonialism, 3, 28, 66, 79, 107, 123
Colossians, Letter to the, 68
conciliar Christology, 7, 13, 19, 47, 59, 61, 63, 94, 97
consubstantiality, 12, 13, 15, 18, 62, 107
Constantine, Emperor, 18
Constantinople, First Council of, 7–8, 18, 22, 97, 121
Constantinople, Second Council of, 120

Index

constructive theology, 11, 13, 77
Corinthians, First Letter to the, 29
cosmic Christology, 9, 19, 68–69, 98, 99, 124
cosmology, 6, 25, 27, 111
cosmos, 5–6, 19, 27, 68, 70, 75, 95–96, 98–99, 106, 123
covenant, 70, 72
creation Christology, 64, 68–72, 74–75, 121, 127
Creator, God as, 18, 22–25, 53–55, 81, 85, 130
creedal Christology, 11, 13
critical retrieval, xii, 77, 91
crucifixion, 69
Cyril of Alexandria, 8, 21–22, 59–61, 77, 107, 120

Darwin, Charles, 25–26, 108
decomposition, 37
deep incarnation, 69, 124, 125
diversity, 56, 90
divine love, 78–80
Docetism, 7
dyophysite Christology, 107

Earth, 24, 49
Earth Bible Project, 99
Ebionite Christology, 7
Ecclesiastes, 56
ecofeminism, 88
ecoliberation, 50
ecological hermeneutics, 99
ecological problems, xi–xii, 91, 117
ecomimetic interpretation, 33–35, 50, 57, 89, 100, 111
ecosystems, 39, 42, 45–46, 49, 57
ecumenical councils, xii, 7, 15, 22, 24, 27–29, 90, 94–95, 97
election, 63, 69–72, 126
environmental degradation, 3, 13, 28, 34, 132
environmental ethics, 126
environmental management, 89
Ephesus, Council of, 7–8, 22, 97, 121
equality, 79

ethics, 88–90
ethnicity, 24, 29
Eusebius of Caesarea, 18, 104
evolution, 25–27, 43, 47, 69, 72
evolutionary biology, 6, 25, 109
extraterrestrial life, 6, 66, 75, 96, 123

Father, God as, 14–15, 17–18, 23, 60, 74, 101, 128
feminism, 28–29, 33–34, 83, 93
forests, 39
fungus, 43

gender, 22–24, 30, 80
Genesis, 21, 55, 115, 119
Gnosticism, 15, 17
Gospels, 3, 5, 11, 14, 95
Great Chain of Being, 49
Greco-Roman philosophy, 14
Gregory of Nazianzus, 20, 105, 106
Gregory of Nyssa, 9, 23–24, 29, 98, 103–5, 107, 116
Gregory the Great, 106, 111

han (Korean concept), 86, 132
Henry of Ghent, 54
hierarchies, 14, 19–21, 35, 41, 79, 82, 100, 119
historical Jesus, 2, 81, 94, 124, 129
homoousios, 14, 17–19, 23–24
human bodies, 27, 49, 57
hypostasis, 18–19

imago Dei (image of God), 21, 28–29, 106, 107, 122
immortality, 15, 17, 61, 65
immutability, 52–54, 56, 58–61
inanimate bodies, 34–37, 49, 67, 69, 79, 111
inclusion, 13, 78
indigenous traditions, 88
infima species, 22, 26, 100
infralapsarianism, 63, 67, 82, 121
injustice, 13, 31, 62, 77
insects, 41–44, 113
intelligence, 40, 44, 46–47

Index

interdependence, 37, 41–49, 56–57, 62, 63, 67–69, 72–73, 81, 83–88, 131
Irenaeus of Lyons, 15–16, 69, 99, 101, 103–5, 124, 128
irrationality, 41, 43
Isaiah, Book of, 115
Israel, 108

James, Letter of, 119
Job, 55
John, Gospel of, 14, 18, 55, 68, 77
Judaism, 14–15, 108
justice, 16, 53, 75, 104, 130, 131
Justin Martyr, 105

kenotic Christology, 80, 95
Kierkegaard, Søren, 105, 114

leaf-cutter ants (*Atta cephalotes*), 41–44, 48, 57, 113, 120
liberation, 28, 53, 86, 87
limestone (biological), 35–37, 44, 48, 57, 67, 69, 111
Logos, 28–29, 124, 128, 129, 130
Luke, Gospel of, 112, 115

Maimonides, 118
maleness, 29–31, 33–34, 83, 110
Marcion, 83
marine life, 37
material bodies, 56, 81, 85, 115
Matthew, Gospel of, 55–56, 112
Maximus the Confessor, 20, 92, 106, 110, 111, 124
medieval theology, 50
metacognition, 46
metaphysics, 72–75, 125, 126–27, 130
microbiology, 25, 27
mind, 20
minerals, 36
mobility, 40
monotheism, 14, 17
mortality, 9, 56, 64–65, 58
mutability, 65, 85
mysticism, 51

Nestorius of Constantinople, 8, 60, 120
Nicaea, First Council of, 2, 7–9, 15, 18–20, 22, 59–60, 62, 97, 100, 121
Nicene Christology, 23, 33–34, 46
Nicene Creed, 1, 13

omnipotence, 52–54
omniscience, 66
orthodoxy, Christian, 17, 104

patriarchy, 13, 28–30, 34, 46, 50, 79, 83, 107
perception, 41, 44
Peter, First Letter of, 123
Philippians, Letter to the, 80, 131
photosynthesis, 36, 38, 49, 111
phronesis (practical wisdom), 89
plankton, 35–36
plants, 35, 38–41, 43, 45, 49, 57, 67, 116, 124
Platonic philosophy, 26, 100, 130
plurality, 57, 63
Pope Paul VI, 92
posthumanism, 108
priesthood, 29–30, 110
process theology, 47, 56, 95
Protestant Christianity, 68, 122, 126
Psalms, 55
Pseudo-Dionysius, 51, 116

quaking aspens (*Populus tremuloides*), 39–40, 112, 119

race, 22–23
racism, xii, 13, 28, 31
rational animals, 44–47
rational soul, 22, 34, 44, 107
rationality, 29–30, 46, 66–67
reconciliation, 15–16, 19, 64–65, 68, 96, 98, 106, 129
relational ontology, 73, 130
reproduction, 9, 38
resurrection, 9, 69, 72, 86, 104, 129
revelation, 5–6, 50, 64, 66, 74–75, 96, 108
Romans, Letter to the, 24, 67, 79, 108, 123

salvation Christologies, 63–68, 121
salvation history, 70
Sankofa bird, xi, 91
scientific research, 25–28, 90, 109
Scotus, Duns, 54, 117, 118
sensation, 40
socio-ecological systems, 48–49
Son of God, 14, 17–18, 23, 59–60, 128
soteriology, 8, 15–16, 18, 83–84, 99
    soteriological models, 16–17, 19, 102, 103
souls, 20–22, 34, 44, 65, 107
Southern Baptist Convention, 2, 93, 96
species, 26–27, 34, 48–49, 56, 79, 88, 100, 108–9, 123
stability, 37, 41, 44, 48, 57
Stoic philosophy, 100
substance, 15–19
superorganism, 43, 49
supralapsarianism, 63, 67, 69–71, 121
symbiosis, 43

taxonomy, 14, 100
Tertullian, 83, 132
theocentrism, 71
theodicy, 69
tradition, xi–xii, 10–11, 91, 111
transcendence, 54–55, 57, 62, 87, 118
transformation, 37, 44, 47–49, 56–58, 63, 65, 85, 88
Trinity, 10, 84, 87–88, 90, 119

unmoved mover, God as, 50

vegetative bodies, 38–41, 112
virgin Mary, 1, 8

western scrub-jays (*Aphelocoma californica*), 44–48, 57, 62, 113, 114
white supremacy, 34, 50, 79